Property

Key Concepts in Political Theory

Property

Robert Lamb

polity

First published in 2021 by Polity Press

Polity Press
65 Bridge Street
Cambridge CB2 1UR, UK

Polity Press
101 Station Landing
Suite 300
Medford, MA 02155, USA

ISBN-13: 978-1-5095-1919-4
ISBN-13: 978-1-5095-1920-0 (pb)

A catalogue record for this book is available from the British Library.

Typeset in 10.5 on 12 pt Sabon
by Fakenham Prepress Solutions, Fakenham, Norfolk NR21 8NL
Printed and bound in Great Britain by CPI Group (UK) Ltd, Croydon

The publisher has used its best endeavours to ensure that the URLs for external websites referred to in this book are correct and active at the time of going to press. However, the publisher has no responsibility for the websites and can make no guarantee that a site will remain live or that the content is or will remain appropriate.

Every effort has been made to trace all copyright holders, but if any have been overlooked the publisher will be pleased to include any necessary credits in any subsequent reprint or edition.

For further information on Polity, visit our website:
politybooks.com

For Lawrence

Contents

Acknowledgements

I am very grateful to George Owers at Polity for first suggesting (in late 2015) that I write this book and for being – along with Julia Davies – supportive and patient as I followed the established academic convention of missing multiple agreed deadlines. I am not in the habit of missing more than one such deadline, but the last four years have been very hectic. Thanks are due to various colleagues and family members, but particularly to whomever developed the 'out-of-office' email message that helped me keep some time to myself during my tenure as head of department, enabling me to make (slow) progress on the manuscript.

Much of what I have learned about property over the years has come from conversations with other scholars. Many of these conversations were at stimulating workshops organised by Chris Pierson, through the Political Studies Association's 'Politics of Property' specialist group that he led so brilliantly. The comments I received on the manuscript from the three anonymous referees (and from three others on the original proposal) were very useful, including objections from one overwrought libertarian critic, which helped persuade me that I was on broadly the right track. Ross Carroll provided valuable comments on the text towards the very end of its composition and I benefited from the excellent copy-editing of Tim Clark. While writing a book that is essentially an introduction to its subject, I have had in mind the two teachers who first introduced me to political philosophy as an undergraduate – Gabriella Slomp and Kevin Francis – with such infectious passion and enthusiasm. Most importantly, as well as providing her typically piercing thoughts on the manuscript, Sarah Drews Lucas helped keep me loved (and sane) as the last years have flown by. This book is dedicated to our son, who was born this week, amidst a global pandemic.

R. L.
Exeter, April 2020

Introduction: What is Property?

In his novel *The Information*, Martin Amis makes the following observations – via his hapless protagonist Richard Tull – about the worldview and attitudes of an artist:

> He was an artist when he saw society: it never crossed his mind that society had to be like this, had any right, had any business being like this. A car in the street. Why? Why *cars*? This is what an artist has to be: harassed to the point of insanity or stupefaction by first principles. (Amis 1995: 11)

Political philosophers are likely to recognise this way of looking at the world. Though political philosophy takes different forms, the perspective Amis ascribes to the artist – that of looking at the social world and asking *why?* – captures one of its most enduring modes. For a great many political philosophers, it is a concern with the *justification* of social and political norms, traditions, institutions, and practices that defines their field of scholarly inquiry. We see this concern with normative questions throughout the history of Western political thought, from the writings of Plato and Aristotle to those of John Rawls and Jürgen Habermas. Political philosophy involves looking at the world and asking why it is organised the way it is and not some other way. It routinely subjects seemingly ordinary and everyday institutions to an intense level of scrutiny and its practitioners experience intense excitement and wonder, though it can occasionally feel like insanity or stupefaction.

In modern, Western liberal democracies, few social institutions are more ordinary and everyday than private property. The extent of its ordinariness is appreciable not only in the way in which people go about their daily business (how so much of our lives depends on the distinction between the things that are *yours* and *mine*), but also in the habitual assumptions of certain academic disciplines. Some scholars – in fields where there is a marked reluctance to acknowledge the inherent contingency and unpredictability in human affairs – accept the existence of exclusive ownership rights as an almost natural phenomenon. As such, they regard the institution as requiring only a descriptive and functional explanation rather than any critical interrogation or normative justification. The attitude of many economists towards property can seem, for instance, to parallel that of a doctor giving an account of a human heart to a layperson: they often appear interested in showing its purpose as a natural part within an organic whole, as though it were fulfilling a kind of evolutionary requirement. The hugely influential analysis of property by the economist Harold Demsetz (1967) typifies this naturalistic approach. Demsetz presents the institution of private ownership as an almost necessary feature of successful economic life, as a sophisticated system that requires an explanation only in terms of the efficient social function we can ascribe to it. For Demsetz, 'a primary function of property rights is that of guiding incentives' (1967: 348) to generate economic advantages from human behaviour. His is a descriptive cost-benefit account of private property deployed to vindicate its existence, so that economists can then more confidently embed it as a necessary feature of their analytic framework. Given his approach to the rationality of private property as he encountered it in the world, it is unsurprising that Demsetz elsewhere complains of a 'nirvana fallacy' within discussions of social institutions, wherein scholars seek to judge them against allegedly idealised standards. Although political philosophers often and increasingly seek to anchor their work in analyses of real world phenomena – eschewing explicit abstract utopianism in favour of addressing urgent social problems – they know that the very idea of a nirvana fallacy places undue restrictions on their theoretical imaginations. The notion of an unavailable nirvana encourages us to defer uncritically to the institutions that surround us and thus allows them to appear as natural features of the world rather than contingent human creations that we can reform, improve, or reject.

We can juxtapose a critical, historicised role for the normative political theorist to the naturalistic tendency we often find in much modern economics as well as other broadly positivistic social sciences. Political philosophy can acknowledge the contingency that characterises all social practices and institutions and invite us to interrogate the world around us in the manner of Amis's artist: it provokes us to ask probing questions about the character of our civic life. In the case of this book, the question we will address is *why private property?* Asking such radical questions does not, of course, in any way rule out conservative conclusions. It does not prevent a compelling justification of the status quo, whatever that may be. The only thing political philosophy really rules out is lazy thinking, which can be either radical or conservative. If the main route to lazy thinking is the denial of contingency in human affairs, then perhaps the best antidote is attention to history. Such attention reveals considerable disagreement about the justifiability of property. Indeed, while the mundane nature of private ownership might make its justification seem an almost self-evident matter for many economists – such that it requires only a cost-benefit analysis and a functional explanation – the history of ideas reveals it to be a perennially controversial idea that divides political opinion violently. On the one hand, many claim that private ownership is a fundamental right and have identified numerous grounds for its legitimacy, including its importance for individual freedom and the wider benefits its existence ensures for the community as a whole. On the other hand, perhaps as many have argued that property is responsible for lamentable levels of poverty and inequality and is therefore unjustifiable as an institution.

In this book, I provide an exposition and assessment of some of the most promising attempts to justify private property and overcome the criticisms levelled against it. Through a truncated and selective tour of historical and contemporary philosophical arguments, I explore some of the most significant theoretical accounts of ownership rights. The selection of theories discussed reflects my judgement about what constitute important and influential philosophical arguments. Constraints of space mean that I cannot cover several important writers who have had interesting things to say about property, but there is an abundance of further reading available for those who wish to explore the topic further.[1]

By the end of our exploration of theories of property, I conclude that private ownership *can* ultimately be justified, though not via the arguments pursued by many of its most ardent cheerleaders. As I present my assessment of the theories at hand, I will focus on their weaknesses as well as their strengths and be clear about which arguments are *incapable* of justifying private property. The explication of political concepts – the way in which they are organised and presented to the reader – inevitably involves the normative commitments of the author. The first step in responsible normative theorising is to realise and acknowledge that we all bring our identities and intellectual baggage on the journey with us. There is no position of pristine detachment from the world available to us and no real ivory tower to which to retreat, though the fantasy of such a possibility does remain a source of comfort to some. To pretend that political theorising is some kind of objective science seems to me, however, to be rather naive and perhaps a symptom of a misplaced scientism that tasks philosophy with more than it could (or should) ever hope to accomplish. It does not, of course, follow from this observation that normative political theory is nothing more than the expression of mere unfiltered opinion, and nor is this book the unfurling of mine. The point is rather that while I offer accurate and robust accounts of each of the theories I consider – and aim to approach them with the scholarly obligation of interpretive charity – it will be obvious that I regard some as superior to others. This acknowledgement should not worry anyone who is encountering political philosophy for the first time, because its mode of inquiry thrives on profound disagreement, often about the most basic theoretical commitments. When you do disagree with me, the best thing to do is therefore to think about why

I am mistaken and where you think my various arguments and/or interpretations unravel, and to do this you will often need to turn to the primary texts themselves, for which there is *never* any substitute.

Contesting concepts

Before we attend to the arguments of either defenders or critics of property, the first and most basic step is to make clear our object of study. We need, in other words, to establish exactly what private property *is*. We need to get a proper grip on the meaning of this key concept before we can justify (or criticise) it. This task is not a straightforward one. The distinction between conceptual explication (what property *is*) and normative justification (why property is valuable) is a potentially slippery one. There is a danger that any account of the conceptual character of property – no matter how stark or ostensibly anodyne – may end up smuggling in features that are highly relevant to its justification. This danger is well worth highlighting from the outset.

Perhaps all concepts are *potentially* capable of having a politically controversial definition. From the sheer contingency of both conceptual meaning (that ideas are changed and developed over time and are open to differing cultural interpretations) and the apparently inexhaustible possibilities for political contestation, it would seem to follow that there are no politically neutral concepts. For example, gorgonzola is widely accepted to be a blue-veined cheese exclusively produced in an established number of Italian areas (in the regions of Lombardy and Piedmont). Its character and geographical identity are defined and policed by a supra-national quality assurance benchmark which is rooted in cultural practices, enshrined by rules, and protected by a legal apparatus. The definition of gorgonzola is nevertheless contingent. There could, in principle, be new provinces added to the list of legitimate producers, or (heaven forfend) the manufacturing process could be changed. Although there would seem to be nothing inherently political about the conceptual meaning of gorgonzola, we can easily see how

its definition could become hotly disputed. We can appreciate that were gorgonzola to be conceptually redefined as
a cheese designated as creatable in Lombardy but *not* in
Piedmont, there would undoubtedly be considerable uproar.
Such a redefinition is nevertheless possible and always has the
potential to be politically controversial. What is at issue in
the definition of such social concepts is not a matter of scientific fact, but of cultural interpretation. There is no such thing
as a politically neutral definition of conceptual meaning: even
the most ordinary concepts are ripe for politicisation.

Though the contingency of meaning obviously broadens
the scope of conceptual contestability, some ideas are
evidently prone to perennial politicisation. One of the most
famous examples is the idea of freedom. There have been
long-standing debates about whether freedom is conceivable
only as the predicate of an action and therefore whether the
relevant obstacles to its exercise must be solely *physical* in
nature. Critics of this familiar, 'negative' understanding of
freedom (associated with the political thought of Thomas
Hobbes) argue that it has normative implications that belie
its ostensible starkness and neutrality. Such a definition of
freedom is, after all, incapable of ruling out the possibility
of merely *threatened* interference as a source of infringement
worth worrying about politically. We can imagine a scenario
wherein an absolute ruler seeks to dominate and control the
behaviour of their subjects through fear, without actually
acting to reduce their physical freedom.[2] According to this
negative conception, if there is no physical interference,
the tyrant in question – no matter what threats have been
issued – has done nothing to limit or curtail the freedom
of his subjects. As Hillel Steiner (1994: 23) observes in his
defence of the negative account of freedom, the great irony
of the line in *The Godfather* when Vito Corleone talks of
making his enemy 'an offer he can't refuse' (to comply or
be killed) is that the victim of the threat could, in principle,
refuse compliance. The fact that there could be such a
refusal supposedly reveals the victim's freedom to be techni-
cally unimpeded by the threat. Putting aside the issue of
its practical, political entailments, the negative definition
of freedom also has theoretical implications through its
crowding out of alternative understandings. It rules out, for

example, a more demanding conception of freedom as a kind of existential condition, which would imply the existence of – and therefore the need for political attention to – potentially mental or cultural as well as material obstacles to its exercise. As long as the negative definition is accepted, discussions about the protection or value of freedom within a community thus proceed without heed to such potential obstacles. The example of freedom indicates just how porous the boundary between conceptual and normative analysis can be. Even the barest conceptual definition can have considerable political resonance.

Philosophical analysis of property likewise disturbs the border between the conceptual and the normative in ways that can be quite glaring. The question *what is property?* cannot be approached innocently. It is practically impossible to define the concept in uncontroversial, apolitical terms, even when the discussion assumes (as ours does) that we are talking about private property specifically, rather than other forms. For example, the right to bequeath an owned holding to another person after death is very often included as a core part of the concept. Yet the ascription of this capacity as a definitive feature of property rights would seem to foreclose, or at the least limit, certain normative questions about the legitimacy of the state acting to tax or redistribute things that are owned. If having the right to bequeath my property is part of what it means to own something, then the case for taxing the transfer becomes a much harder sell. On the other hand, any decision to *deny* that the concept of property includes the power to bequeath – and instead assume that individuals do not have such rights to hold against the redistributive authority of the state – appears just as guilty of smuggling an equivalent normative claim into an austerely analytic definition. If the right to bequeath property is not part of what it means to own it, there seems no obvious argument against its taxation or even confiscation following the owner's death.[3] Questions about the meaning of private property thus inescapably intrude on questions about its fair distribution. In doing so, they invite consideration of other political concepts, such as freedom, justice, and equality, which will make various appearances during our subsequent discussions.

There is then no neat separation between conceptual definition and normative theorising, and this is particularly apparent when it comes to the most perennially contested ideas in political thought. We nevertheless do need to settle on some basic working definition of private property as a social institution, if only to distinguish it from other concepts, such as freedom (and gorgonzola). Merely pointing out the politically problematic nature of ascribing meaning to everyday concepts is surely not the only role that political theory can play in our discussions of them. While it cannot provide any detached or even final adjudication between rival contestations of the authoritative meanings of normative concepts, political theorising can point us towards grounds for endorsing some understandings over others, by interrogating both the premises such theories depend upon and the implications that they entail. The theories and arguments selected for discussion in this book represent a desire to both own up to the necessary mingling of conceptual analysis with the normative claims involved in substantive political theory, while also making the case for some accounts of property being more attractive than others. The material covered herein serves this dual function because it is, for the most part, *historical* in nature.

An historical approach to the concept of property

There are many good reasons to study the history of political ideas. Two of them are particularly germane to the discussion of key concepts. On the one hand, the history of ideas impresses the sheer contingency and contestability of our political inheritance upon us. It indicates that others have construed the concepts that define our civic debates as having different meanings and implications in divergent contexts. On the other hand, the history of ideas also reminds of us of the perennial nature of political debate. It reveals that conceptual contestations in alien historical contexts often concern the same ideas that animate our own political discussions. The upshot of these two contrasting but entwined phenomena (the contingent and the perennial) is that they provide the student of the history of ideas with a rich treasure of fascinating arguments – some familiar and some alien to our civic culture – about the concepts that we deploy in our contemporary political conversations.

An historical approach to property also, in my view, allows us to bypass a contemporary philosophical dispute concerning the nature of property as a concept. This dispute turns on whether the concept of property has any essential characteristics. Some theorists argue that there is a stable and definite conceptual core to the idea of property. James Penner, for instance, suggests that the idea of *exclusive use* provides the 'formal essence of the right' to own property. According to this understanding, 'the right to property is a right to exclude others from things which is grounded by the interest we have in the use of things' (Penner 1997: 71, emphasis suppressed). As Penner points out, the concepts of exclusion and use often come together through ownership rights: we are accustomed to thinking of private property as implying our legitimate need or desire to use a particular thing and, correspondingly, requiring that we are able to exclude others from doing so. This combination of exclusion and use does not mean that our ownership rights obtain only in our particular occasions of use – our furniture does not cease belonging to us when we are not immediately using it. The idea of exclusive use signals instead the connection between our rightfully owned property and our purposiveness and intentionality. It captures the fact that property is valuable to us because of the role it plays in our lives, as part of our long-term personal projects. On this construal, property confers a series of benefits on its owner through the exercise of certain liberties. She can, without interference, share, transfer, or derive benefit from, the property in question, as well as enter into various forms of contract concerning it.

We can immediately see that this account of the essential meaning of property is quite explicitly at once conceptual and normative: it makes plain that the view advanced about the nature of property (exclusion) derives from its justifiable purpose (the interests served by its use). The important point is, however, that property is understood here as a discernible and unified idea with a definitive conceptual core. This 'unified thesis', and the analysis that underpins it, has some clear intuitive purchase – it seems to describe successfully how we might think of property in our everyday lives, when we stop and consider it. It seems easy to get our heads around the notion that the right to a chair is explained via the benefits involved in being able to use it however we please and, furthermore, that the practical manifestation of this benefit is my entitlement to control the exclusion of others from interfering with it. Despite its intuitive pull, however, the view of property as having an essential conceptual core – whether defined by exclusive use or anything else – has fallen into some measure of scholarly disrepute in recent years.

The most influential way of thinking about property in contemporary legal philosophy instead abandons altogether the view of it as a *singular* concept, and understands it instead to be a 'bundle' of discrete and separable legal relations. There have been different ways of conceiving exactly what such a bundle entails, but the basic idea is that we can endeavour to separate the various sticks that comprise it and, in so doing, acquire a better understanding of the nature of the legal and social phenomena at issue. Proponents of the bundle approach claim that it clears away what they regard as a fog of conflation that blinds political and legal discussion of the subject. To appreciate the thinking behind the bundle theory, we need to step back a bit and go over some of the key features of rights themselves. Beyond their expressive, political purposes – which might include the recognition of our dignity or moral standing in a community – rights serve to enable and prohibit our freedoms, making some actions permissible and others impermissible. In the context of property, this function seems straightforward and relates back to our interest in having systematic and permanent protection for specific resources, which become our holdings rather than those of anyone else.

Perhaps even more fundamental to the understanding of rights is their *relational* nature. Rights delineate realms of permissible action *between* individuals and therefore make sense only in a social context: we hold rights *against* others. Property rights govern relations between persons (and corporations) rather than between persons (and corporations) and specific things. In a world with only one person (but lots of things) the idea of property rights would presumably be superfluous because the relevant relational context would not exist: there would be no other individual against whom to hold rights. This aspect of rights can help us be wary of some of the confusing language that we are prone to use when talking about ownership. We might talk of the right I have *over* my magnifying glass, but it is a mistake to believe that this right is somehow *held against* the inanimate object, rather than against the other agents within my socio-legal sphere.

Not all of the conventional legal relations traditionally associated with the concept of property ownership are, strictly speaking, *rights*. Philosophers generally follow Wesley Hohfeld's (1919) understanding of rights as *claims*, which are characterised by their correlative concept, *duties*. Rights of this sort imply duties held by others. If the right I have over my teapot is a right in the sense of a claim, then it implies a correlative duty in others to respect – and forbear from interference with – my ownership of it. Put crudely, my property right means that, under most circumstances, you are *obliged* to keep your hands off my stuff and that the relevant legal authority, if required, can enforce this obligation. Not all rights are claims in this sense. It would be unusual to interpret the right to free speech, for example, as a claim that generates a corresponding duty for others. Such a right does not conventionally imply any corresponding obligation that prevents any person from interfering with its exercise, perhaps by talking over you, or otherwise distracting your audience as you address them. Rights to both engage in and disrupt free speech would seem to co-exist coherently, without duties of non-interference appearing on the scene. It arguably makes more sense to construe free speech as what Hohfeld terms a *privilege* (or liberty) right, which correlates not to obligations but merely to the privileges held by others. When a person has a privilege to undertake an action, what this means is that they are under no duty to refrain from it: privileges are essentially (negative) freedoms to undertake actions without fear of penalty, but they do not entail protective duties imposed on others to enable those actions.

While it might seem obviously true that property rights are claim rights with implied duties of non-interference held by others, thinking of ownership as a bundle of discrete legal relations complicates this view. My ownership of a teapot may customarily involve my right to exclusive use of it, but it may also include more than this, or it might come with certain conditions or limitations attached. In addition to my right to use, my ownership will likely also include any number of what Hohfeld refers to as *powers*. In the Hohfeldian framework, a power means the ability to transform legal relationships. My ownership right may incorporate, for example, the power of transmissibility, wherein I (as owner) can decide to give you my teapot – and the bundle of entitlements that come with it – through an exchange or, after I die, as a bequest.

In an influential essay on the meaning of property, A. M. Honoré lists eleven 'standard ingredients of ownership', and thus identifies some of the conceptual sticks that we might expect to find in our bundle of rights. According to him:

> Ownership comprises the right to possess, the right to use, the right to manage, the right to the income of the thing, the right to the capital, the right to security, the rights or incidents of transmissibility and absence of term, the prohibition of harmful use, liability to execution, and the incident of residuarity. (Honoré 1993: 370)

One of Honoré's key observations is that it is not necessary for *all* of these legal relations to be present for a status of ownership to obtain. Having a property right can mean different things in different contexts – we should not expect all bundles to look alike in terms of the particular sticks they contain. An implication of this observation is that several of the listed relations are sufficient conditions for the existence of ownership. We can, Honoré thinks, make sense of a person owning a plot of land without her having any corresponding power to bequeath it to whomever she pleases. His list of possible relations of ownership suggests some flexibility in its understanding and does much to help illustrate the bundle theory of property. The upshot of the bundle thesis is to shift our focus to the discrete sticks within it and expose each to its own analysis. What we might think of as ownership becomes reducible to its elemental parts, which may themselves have different moral, political, or legal justifications. A focus on the bundle of rights involved in a particular set of legal relations reveals the contingency of their relationship to each other: a person's right to occupy a plot of land has no necessary connection with any coincident right to transfer it. Whether these individual relations happen to co-exist on a specific occasion arguably tells us nothing about any discernible idea of property as a unified whole. We can easily envisage situations of ownership existing with bundles of fewer or different entitlements.

An entailment of the bundle thesis – and perhaps one of the motivations driving its advocacy – is that the very notion of property as a singular object of study is a product of mistaken, mystified thought. Reference to an overarching concept of ownership would seem to posit an illusory unity to what is not actually one, but numerous legal relationships. We cannot consider such relationships as constituting any kind of singular entity without incurring important misunderstandings of their natures, justifications, and implications. On the bundle account, it makes no sense to analyse ownership as an institution and we should attend instead to specific practices like the *right to use* or *the power to transfer*. The concept of property thus vanishes out of sight, with the notion of an *owner* a misleading oversimplification, perhaps even a category error, with no possible basis in reality.[4] It emerges as a fiction, a weirdly inaccurate kind of shorthand device that encourages the reification of a popular idea that blinds us to a proper understanding of social and legal phenomena.

The bundle theory of property might appear irresistible. It does always seem possible, after all, to separate the idea of property out into distinct legal relations, such that our everyday notion of ownership slips away. The view that exclusive use is capable of serving as the conceptual core of property is obviously impossible to square with the compelling nature of the bundle thesis of property, which implies that giving a central place to use (or any other imagined essence) is a somewhat arbitrary stipulation that will not do the work required of it. In spite of the dominance of the bundle approach – that pushes us to avoid talk of *the* concept of ownership altogether – I think that it does make sense to continue to invoke property as a legitimate and fruitful focus for our theoretical attention. An historical approach to political ideas allows us to sidestep debates about the meaning of property, or indeed of any other contested political concept. We can avoid the culs-de-sac of a conceptual essentialism on the one hand, and a denial of meaning on the other, by thinking of property as a cluster of contingently related ideas that comprises an historical tradition of thought. On this understanding, the following chapters are not about property in the sense of a singular concept that stands outside, or stretches across, time, but are rather concerned with rival *conceptions* of property that together form an intellectual tradition, and include the various and discrete relationships highlighted by the bundle theory.

In this book, I highlight important parts of the tradition of thinking and arguing about property. I examine and assess conceptions and normative contestations of property advanced by different individuals, who are often in direct conversation with each other. We will consider each of these theories on their own terms, insofar as the discussion will not assume an established definition of property to compare against their individual understandings. Such an author-centred analysis avoids cementing intellectual traditions into rigid ideologies. Although I will regularly invoke political or theoretical traditions – libertarianism, utilitarianism, anarchism, and so on – I use these labels loosely; as I will make clear, Nozick's theory does not *exhaust* the libertarian theory of property and Bentham's does not *define* the utilitarian alternative. No individual theory of property is reducible to the intellectual tradition of which it is part or the political ideology it is supposed to represent.[5]

Structure of the book

In this chapter, I have raised the thorny issue of defining property as a key concept in political theory. I discussed two contrasting ways of thinking about property: the view that it has an essential conceptual core and the view that it is a misleading notion analysable only when broken down into discrete and specific legal relations. My suggestion is that despite the appeal of the bundle theory, property remains a comprehensive and very powerful point of navigation through a set of ideas, comprising a discernible lineage of political argument. Indeed, as we will see below, various political writers – across philosophical traditions – have sought to define, theorise, and contest the idea of property, even where they disagree about its precise nature.

The structure of the rest of the book is as follows. In the first chapter, I consider why we might think that private property stands in need of a compelling justification. To explain the urgency of this undertaking – beyond the aforementioned habit of political philosophers surveying the world and asking why it is the way it is – I introduce some of the most radical dismissals of the legitimacy of property ownership in Western political thought. After outlining the dramatic critique advanced in the eighteenth century by Jean-Jacques Rousseau, I briefly consider the case against property put forward by writers in the anarchist and socialist traditions, focusing on the thought of Pierre-Joseph Proudhon and William Morris. Much of the case against private property concerns the severe poverty and inequalities that are associated with a world of *yours* and *mine*, as well as the claimed appeal of the radically different world that we can imagine without it.

The remainder of the book is a response to this challenge posed by the claimed illegitimacy of private ownership. In the following five chapters, I consider various theoretical attempts to justify property as an institution. In the second and third chapters, I examine an account of ownership within the libertarian tradition, focusing on the construal of property as an inviolable right that implies the wrongness of coercive taxation. I first analyse Robert Nozick's libertarian political theory, showing how his radical defence of property rights against the state is derivative ultimately from a principle of *self-ownership* rather than from a commitment to freedom. In the following chapter I uncover the roots of self-ownership through a discussion of the history of the supposed ancestry of libertarian thought (in early modern and modern natural rights theories). I show that, within these historical theories, property rights have traditionally been justified through reference to an overarching account of natural law. My suggestion is that, when unmoored from this account, the modern, secularised principle of self-ownership looks eccentrically individualistic and incapable of sustaining the radical political conclusion advanced by Nozick. While the most obvious place to find a justification for property might seem to be within the libertarian tradition, my suggestion is that philosophers must look elsewhere.

In the fourth and fifth chapters, I consider alternative justifications for property ownership that do not try to defend the institution through reference to natural rights. I look first at the consequentialist accounts of the institution we find in the utilitarian tradition, in the writings of David Hume, Jeremy Bentham, and J. S. Mill. Each uses the idea of utility in a different way to justify the institution of property ownership and its associated legal conventions. After a discussion of the logics that drive them, I conclude that these three different justifications – though they are arresting and again have some intuitive pull – seem likewise incapable of providing a solid foundation for the existence of private property, their vulnerability traceable to the empirical claims upon which they must rely. I then move on, in the fifth chapter, to outline what might be the most compelling justification of private property in modern political thought. This justification, which can be found in the political writing of nineteenth-century German philosopher G. W. F. Hegel, is one that takes seriously the meaning and purpose of property in both its individual and social dimensions. The attraction of the Hegelian justification is, I suggest, that it can account for both the individualistic nature of the institution of private ownership and its ultimately social justification, while being unaffected by the vagaries that would threaten any consequentialist version.

However, while Hegel might provide a convincing account of *why* property exists, and the *forms* that it can take, his account is not without difficulties. For one thing, his theory raises the problems of poverty, inequality, and intergenerational injustice – issues on which Hegel is either silent or offers answers that are less than satisfactory.

There is something missing from his overall theory that is addressable through a more holistic normative framework. I therefore turn, in the sixth chapter, to consider the case for such a holistic approach, in relation to what John Rawls has termed 'property-owning democracy'. Rawls's theory embeds his commitment to property ownership within his broader account of justice, and does so in a way that fuses liberal commitments to freedom and equality. My ultimate conclusion is that private property can indeed be justified as a social institution, but its value as a concept is articulable and appreciable through an overall normative philosophical framework, rather than in isolation. To reach that point, we need to embark on quite a journey. We must first begin, however, by considering the view that the journey is not worth undertaking at all, on the basis that we should reject private property from the outset as an indefensible political institution.

1
The Case against Private Property

The bulk of this book will be devoted to discussion of the case for property rights, put forward as part of different political theories. We will focus on various arguments that try to justify private property as a social institution, and examine theories that seek to explain the purpose and value of a world of *yours* and *mine*. Before we discuss the various philosophical arguments advanced in defence of private ownership, however, we will first consider its *critics*. This might seem like a backwards approach to the matter at hand, but my intention is to heighten the interest of the topic by bringing its controversial status into sharp relief. Though property may seem like an ordinary and everyday concept – one that we often take for granted as a mundane fact of our existence in Western societies living with advanced capitalism – its justification is both important and urgent. We can get a sense of the need for a compelling justification for property – beyond the compulsion of the political philosopher to subject all aspects of social life to critical interrogation – by taking a brief look at some of the most provocative arguments against its very existence. Some political thinkers have found property to be, at best, without convincing justification and, at worst, a force for evil in the world. Private ownership has long been an object of critique, damned as a source of injustice and misery by a number of writers in the modern anarchist and socialist traditions. That said, we have only limited space, so I will focus on just three modern political writers who offer stinging critiques of property rights: Jean-Jacques Rousseau, Pierre-Joseph Proudhon, and William Morris.

Jean-Jacques Rousseau

Worries about the legitimacy of private ownership pre-date the rise of industrial capitalism. The emergence of commercial society in the eighteenth century saw critics of private property advance arguments that remain prescient. In his *Discourse on the Origin and Foundations of Inequality* (1754), Jean-Jacques Rousseau assembles one of the most strident and influential philosophical broadsides against private property and the form of society that its existence begets. The tremendous force of Rousseau's critique lies in its weaving together of two distinct and powerful claims: his analysis points, on the one hand, to the unwanted consequences caused by the existence of property and, on the other, to the highly dubious origins of the institution.[1] Apologists for commercial society, he thinks, ignore both of these truths. Rousseau's starting point is the phenomenon of inequality, which is, for him, an obvious fact about the world, and is lamentable because of how it has thwarted human freedom and well-being. His task in the *Discourse* is to identify the factors that cause this inequality and perpetuate the radical material and cultural differences of wealth and poverty that pervade modernity. One of Rousseau's most innovative claims is that these inequalities have no natural basis. On the contrary, for him, the emergence of inequality is an inescapably *social* problem: it is a product of society and not a natural fact. The phenomenon of inequality as we encounter it in civil society is absent from what Rousseau sees as the pre-modern, 'savage' state, where notions of 'need, greed, oppression, desires, and pride' cannot be found (Rousseau 1997a: 132). Contrary to philosophers like Hobbes – who view life without political authority as extremely dangerous because of our innate egoism – Rousseau suggests that the state of human existence that precedes socialisation is mostly peaceful.

In his examination of 'natural man', Rousseau seems to indicate that it is not so much what the savage state had, as what it *lacked*, that explains the absence of inequality. And one of the things it lacked was private property. Rousseau insists that the very establishment of individuated, private ownership as an institution helped create, and then nurture, an inequality of materials, status, and spirit. In a famous passage of the *Discourse*, he makes the following declaration:

> The first man who, having enclosed a piece of ground, to whom it occurred to say, *this is mine*, and found people sufficiently simple to believe him, was the true founder of civil society. How many crimes, wars, murders, how many miseries and horrors Mankind would have been spared by him who, pulling up the stakes or filling in the ditch, had cried out to his kind: Beware of listening to this impostor; You are lost if you forget that the fruits are everyone's and the Earth no one's. (Rousseau 1997a: 161)

Rousseau immediately acknowledges that the impulse towards private acquisition did not come out of nowhere but required the existence of 'prior ideas' that were friendly to selfishness and corruption. The institutional manifestation of the privatisation of ownership nevertheless marks a crucial point of degradation in modernity. The acceptance of the legitimacy of private ownership is, he thinks, the harbinger of a distinct stage in the securement of inequality and, correspondingly, of human misery, and a welcoming invitation to the 'crimes, wars, murders' that have come to characterise our social lives.

For Rousseau, it is not the mere fact that one person encloses land to the *exclusion* of someone else that is at issue. Indeed, *material* inequality is only one part of his story. Rousseau's thesis is ultimately about the transformative psychological development undergone by humans with the emergence of commercial society. As well as legitimising quantitative differences in owned possessions, the establishment of private property cements an *ethos* of inequality in society. An inequality of natural resources mutates quickly into a more insidious inequality of status and power. Social relations become characterised by the dominance of the wealthy over the destitute and needy, who lack moral dignity and struggle for economic subsistence. The rich are, however, not really much better off, as their luxurious desires render them corrupt, and their pride and social mores enslave them. The spirit of inequality ultimately perpetuates itself through the legal and political apparatus. The wealthy, devoid of genuine virtue, become selfishly motivated to establish laws of justice that serve their interests and protect their ownership. They know that 'since [their property rights] had been acquired solely by force, force could deprive them of them without their having reason for complaint' (Rousseau 1997a: 172), and so a robust punitive system is required to secure their holdings and maintain their status.

The other powerful Rousseauian contention is that the initial act of acquisition was itself thievery and therefore the whole institution of private ownership – continued through property transfer, inheritance, and so on – has no legitimate foundation. If Rousseau's historical argument about unjustified appropriation is correct, then this would surely have ramifications that go far beyond his eighteenth-century context. After all, if the first instance of ownership was an illegitimate acquisition and amounted to institu-tionalised theft, then all transactions that stem from this initial violation are perhaps likewise tainted. Although the connection between that very first act of enclosure and my exclusive rights over the coffee table that I have purchased seems at first to be non-existent, the legitimacy of the latter might actually hinge on that of the former. It is troubling to think that the rights we assume and rely on during our daily lives might be the latest link in a chain of historical wrongs.

Is Rousseau correct in his assertion about the ignominious origins of property ownership? In many respects, the answer must be that we simply do not know the true story behind the earliest of *all* property acquisitions. We do know enough about the nature of colonial expansion, however, to be able to assert with confidence that, at the time at which settlers forced various indigenous peoples off their land, huge parts of the world were essentially stolen. When, in the late seventeenth century, John Locke writes 'in the beginning all the World was *America*' (1988: 301), he refers to what he regards as its unspoilt nature. In the context of his theory of property – which we will discuss further in subsequent chapters – he means that at one point in time, the whole world had not been subject to private enclosure, and so was not yet a site of ownership rights. America was, for Locke, unused and unclaimed, and therefore available for appropriation and the establishment of property rights. We know now, of course, that Locke's perspective on the virginal status of America was a colonial one, which denied relevant moral standing – and corresponding political legitimacy – to its indigenous people, whose conceptions of property did not cohere with his own worldview.[2] Modern colonialism – not just in America, but in Africa, Australasia, and elsewhere – demonstrates how many examples there are throughout the world of chains of established property ownership beginning with not merely theft, but also the accompanying mass killing or violent displacement of indigenous peoples. The fact of colonialism, however, does not yet *necessarily* render illegitimate the property rights that have passed through several generations since its violence. We still need to undertake an assessment of the justifications canvassed in the history of political ideas before we could reach such a conclusion. Nevertheless, the undeniable reality of colonialism does very much underscore why the justificatory burden falls on the defender of private ownership, as well as why such a burden is a sizeable and politically urgent one.

The challenge that Rousseau sets out in the *Discourse* is stark: how can property be justified when its existence is responsible for subsequent 'miseries and horrors'? The implication of his analysis – especially given the pure fiat that he thinks underpins its initial establishment – would seem to be that property is nothing more than institutionalised robbery. Rousseau asks the proprietor in modernity, 'Do you know that a great many of your brothers perish or suffer from need of what you have in excess, and that you required the express and unanimous consent of Humankind to appropriate for yourself anything from the common subsistence above and beyond your own?' (1997a: 172). If modernity emerges as corrupt and miserable because of the privatisation of ownership, the corresponding entailment would seem to be towards the rightness of a kind of communist society in which the fruits of the earth belong to everyone, and where any one of whom can draw upon them when necessary. As we will see later, this is not actually the conclusion Rousseau himself reaches, but his analysis did inspire other political writers towards it.

Proudhon and the anarchist case against property

Rousseau's political philosophy had a profound influence on subsequent writers in the anarchist and socialist traditions, many of whom were even more radical in their diagnoses of, and remedies for, the economic ills that they ascribed to private property. The French nineteenth-century anarchist writer Pierre-Joseph Proudhon is one such figure whose work further develops Rousseau's social criticism.[3] Although he embraced various political positions throughout his life, Proudhon's perhaps most iconic text, *What is Property?* (1840), offers a relentless critique of private ownership, rejecting a large number of argumentative strategies traditionally invoked in its justification. For Proudhon, property and poverty are, at once, opposites in their nature, and yet also mutually dependent on each other for their existence: the presence of one implies that of the other. Much of Proudhon's key text is devoted to criticising numerous popular accounts of the origin of private ownership, each of which he regards as bogus. He rejects as implausible a variety of arguments that attempt to explain the emergence of legitimate acquisition through reference to rights gained either by *first occupancy*, or through the *universal consent of humankind*. He shares with later post-colonial critics the view that such narratives are nothing more than offensive fictions. There are, for Proudhon, no grounds for ascribing ownership of a particular portion of land to a person simply because they were its first occupant, and he thinks there is no way universal consent was ever sought – let alone secured – by proprietors at any stage in history.

The origins of the institution of private property are, according to Proudhon, not ancient or pre-historical, but assuredly modern. Furthermore, he thinks that the political validation of property takes place significantly later than Rousseau claimed. Private ownership becomes a fundamental right only with the French Revolution. The Revolutionary spirit – with its well-known commitment to the political trinity of liberty, equality, and fraternity – is, for him, imbued with a fundamental individualism that explicitly accommodates the privatisation of property rights, and the exclusion of the many from ownership. Thus, although the French Declaration of the Rights of Man and of the Citizen venerated equality as a moral axiom, in reality such professions masked a hypocrisy. That document and its constitutional successors failed completely to explain what the professed 'equality before the law' amounted to, and within such an abstract idea lay possibilities for substantive inequalities. For Proudhon, these egalitarian constitutional documents 'assume an *inequality in fortune and status* incompatible with even a shadow of equality in rights' (1994: 29). The collective 'people' – who were the supposed subjects of what he saw as an empty, ineffective constitutional egalitarianism – ended up falling back into the unequal states of 'privilege and servitude' that they held prior to the fall of the *Ancien Régime* (30). A genuinely substantive commitment to equality demands not the affirmation but the rejection of private ownership. Proudhon thus not only rejects the legitimacy of property because of its undesirable consequences – that its existence produces demonstrably terrible hardship, poverty, and inequality – but also because its justification relies on a premise that contains within it an egalitarian principle that actually demands its abolition and in its place the secured freedom of the individual. The existence of private ownership vitiates any claimed formal freedoms. Property is thus, according to Proudhon, (1) unacceptable on consequentialist grounds, and (2) self-contradictory in its justification, which invokes both equality and freedom but delivers neither.

The stated task of Proudhon's intervention is to show that 'every imaginable argument made on behalf of property, no matter what it may be, always and necessarily leads to equality, that is, to the negation of property' and thus demonstrates its lack of justification (1994: 33). In the fourth chapter of *What is Property?*, Proudhon offers ten propositions intended to demonstrate what he terms the 'impossibility' of property: how it is – regardless of its origins – 'a contradiction, a chimera' (117). Several of these propositions look somewhat eccentric and dated to twenty-first-century eyes, as they depend on certain ideas of mathematical proof and economic formulae, as, for instance, with his assumptions about the necessarily changing costs of production and about the nature of capital itself. Other claims remain, however, quite pointed, such as his assertion of the necessary connection between the existence of property and political tyranny.

For Proudhon, in a society in which property is a fundamental right protected by the state, political authority is radically unequal in its distribution, with power following ownership. He bemoans the 'regime of property', under which democracy becomes a sham, with political influence tracking ownership, such that the person who has title to a large amount has the equivalent of 'several hundred votes, while another [without such property] has only one' (1994: 157). According to Proudhon, 'if the sovereignty of each citizen can and should be proportional only to his property, it follows that the small stockholders are at the mercy of the larger ones' and therefore 'property is incompatible with political and civic equality' (157–8). This argument might appear directed at a radically inegalitarian *distribution* of property, rather than at ownership itself: there seems to be no reason why the right to private property must generate vast inequalities of the sort that distort the distribution of political power and threaten democracy. Proudhon disagrees. He thinks that in liberal societies where it is an individualised private right, the nature of property is such that the entitlement to it becomes inviolable and the corresponding inequalities in its distribution therefore unavoidable.

At the same time – and more explicitly in his some of his later works – Proudhon opposes any alternative account of property that imagines the viability of some kind of centralised distributive power capable of maintaining equality. He defends instead an anti-statist form of anarchism or libertarian socialism – often called 'mutualism' – with a kind of marketplace in which workers essentially own their labour. Only through such a regime can individuals find genuine freedom and fulfilment. Proudhon's view of human nature is perhaps less positive than that found in Rousseau's depiction of 'savage man', but he does offer a detailed account of the conditions under which individuals flourish within societies. In advancing his anarchist political theory, he puts forward a developmental account of human sociability, with three key stages. The final stage of his account is characterised by a feeling of 'equity', something that is unobservable in non-human animals: it is a combination of 'generosity, gratitude, ... and friendship' (1994: 183) and drives individual motivation. It is this feeling of equity that compels us 'to seek community with our fellows' with the aim of securing 'equality in the products of nature and of labour' (184). Any society that enables private ownership thus, in Proudhon's view, inevitably prevents individuals from fully flourishing. Property, with its inegalitarian logic of possessive individualism, prevents us from becoming our best selves and properly realising political community. Hence Proudhon demands that we reject it as a matter of moral and political urgency.

Socialism and the idea of life without private ownership

Like anarchism, the socialist tradition is replete with arguments against private property. We often find such arguments embedded within systematic critical analyses of capitalistic economic systems as a whole. Whether implicitly or explicitly, defenders of capitalism tend to accept the sanctity of private ownership rights and regard any alternative property regime as involving a command economy. It is thus not a surprise that a rejection of private property often accompanies a rejection of market economics. Karl Marx is, without question, the most notorious critic of capitalism in the history of political thought, and his influence on socialist economic analysis has been profound. He sought to advance a 'scientific' socialist critique, so described to differentiate it from utopian alternatives. In fact, Marx cited his 'dislike for sentimental socialistic day-dreams' as the only point on which he claimed to be in complete agreement with Proudhon, whose analyses of capitalism he otherwise scorned as based on a superficial and inaccurate understanding of historical facts and processes (Marx 1972a: 142).

The defining thesis of Marx's theory of *historical materialism* is that the economic base of a society (how its 'relations of production' are owned and organised) has a determinative force over its ideational 'superstructure' (its political, legal, and moral institutions and character). This priority of the economic base over the ideological/political superstructure – whereby the nature of the former can explain the nature of the latter – has two relevant implications for thinking about property. The first is that the specific property regime within a society is comprehensible only as a subset of its broader economic arrangements. Thus, in capitalist societies – unlike feudal ones – the ownership of economic power belongs to the ruling capitalist class (the bourgeoisie), who exploit those excluded from such power (the proletariat) by compelling them to sell their labour for less than its true value in order to subsist. The second relevant implication of Marx's materialist thesis is that any projected attempt to give property a normative justification using the tools of political philosophy is likely to be doomed from the start. The reason for this is that normative justifications are *themselves* inevitably superstructural and are therefore not credible as arguments with any independent force. The moral arguments put forward in defence of the right to private property are – as, in the case of the French Revolution, where Marx again agrees with Proudhon – destined to be nothing more than the *ideological* expressions of a class interest they inevitably serve to support. The inviolable right to private ownership is therefore not really grounded in an abstract commitment to liberty or equality, but rather in the very real need for the bourgeoisie to establish a moral (and legal) code to secure its interests. The theories of property advanced from John Locke to Robert Nozick are not assessable as right or wrong, but are comprehensible only as an expression of their class, which, in turn, is explicable through the economic relations reigning at the relevant time. An implication of this thesis is, of course, that any moral case *against* private property will likewise be nothing more than the expression of class interest. There is seemingly no space for authoritative normative political theory within Marx's framework.

For Marx, the class struggle between the bourgeoisie and the proletariat will eventually lead to the revolutionary overthrow of the capitalist economic system and its replacement with some kind of communist alternative. Such an overthrow is the historical purpose of the proletariat. In *The Communist Manifesto* (1848), Marx and Engels assert straightforwardly that 'the theory of the Communists may be summed up in the single sentence: Abolition of private property' (1972c: 484). Yet while Marx's case against private property – as a mere bourgeois right, the existence of which reveals much about the class structure of the society in question – will be compelling for those who accept historical materialism and its corresponding thesis about the necessarily ideological nature of moral claims, it will leave everyone else unmoved. His framework has nothing much to say about a normative theory of property, other than that its prospects are irredeemably bleak. Of course, by intimating that Marx's views on property are of limited interest to us – because of his relegation of normative argument to the status of ideology – I do not mean to imply that the concept was not extremely important to him. He evidently believes that there is much *explanatory* work for the scientific socialist theorist of property to do and offers numerous highly interesting theses on how developments in practices of ownership relate to developments in the legal and political apparatuses (e.g. Marx 1972b: 186–8). Property is, in many respects, at the heart of his economic and political analysis, albeit in a way that departs from our focus on its possible justifiability.

What the abolition of property means for Marx is less clear than in the case of Proudhon. Marx does not provide much in the way of detail about what his own vision of communism looks like; though perhaps disappointing, this omission is not so surprising, as merely painting pictures of life without property is exactly what he wanted his form of scientific socialism to dispense with. Marx's writing was nevertheless a hugely important influence on various nineteenth-century socialists who *did* continue to depict what a society without private ownership might look like. One iconic example of this influence is the thought of the designer, novelist, and craftsperson, William Morris, who founded the Socialist League in Britain in 1884.[4] He was committed to activism and education, though his political writing was markedly different from that of Marx, particularly in its open embrace of utopianism. While Morris's fictional work *News from Nowhere* (1890) might be viewed as exactly the sort of idealised day-dreaming that Marx and so many of his followers have disparaged, its philosophical and political purpose can be found in one of its last lines, when the protagonist reflects on the purpose of his adventures. 'Go back' from your utopian imaginings, he concludes – in the voice of one of the figures encountered during the story – 'and be the happier for having seen us, for having added a little hope to your struggle' (Morris 2003: 181–2).

As well as serving to galvanise and invigorate the hopeful spirits of fellow travellers, *News from Nowhere* is comprehensible as an attempt to outline the 'higher stage' of communist society that was never fully expressed in *The Communist Manifesto* or elsewhere. One of the reasons critics make much of Marx's failure to specify the nature of communistic life is because it is, as noted earlier, quite hard to imagine our lives without private property. Having said that, it is also true that living without property is not *that* hard to imagine and, in this respect, Morris helps us along very well. He also helps himself to a more Rousseauian understanding of human nature than many readers will be willing to accept, because they may conclude that his vision depicts a life of communism too rosily. The key point, however, of Rousseau's approach to the issue of human nature is *not* that individuals are naturally good and capable of harmonious living – as opposed to irredeemably selfish, as someone like Hobbes would counter – but rather that their beliefs, attitudes, and behaviours are contingent, malleable, and therefore improvable. It is this idea of the *malleability* of human nature that Morris appeals to and invokes in *News from Nowhere*. In his utopian socialist society, human attitudes and behaviours differ radically from those we find under capitalism.

Morris's protagonist – William Guest – awakens to find himself in a future society, the members of which have the apparently perfect freedom to do as they please. The people he encounters behave with largely impeccable friendliness, courtesy, and kindness. They partake in whatever work they choose, under no compulsion, and only labour insofar as they *enjoy* the process and the products it creates. Their fulfilling lives mean that they are happy and live longer, with more vigour; older members display more youthful physical appearances than one would expect given their age, and the inhabitants generally reveal more optimistic and grateful attitudes during their interactions with William than do those of his own society. In this utopian society, no schools are required to educate children and there are no prisons because it has abandoned punishment as a largely unnecessary and, in any case, counter-productive practice. There is no government – again unnecessary – and no divorce, because there is no longer any tradition of marriage that would require individuals to commit themselves to one person for the whole of their lives.

Along with the cheerful abandonment of these conventions, there is no individualised, private ownership in Morris's utopia, and its absence pervades every sphere of social intercourse. As William observes, 'my drive from Hammersmith to Bloomsbury, and all the quiet happy life I had seen so many hints of ... would have been enough to tell me that "the sacred rights of property," as we used to think of them, were no more' (2003: 48–9). The lack of such ownership rights and the secured happiness of this newfound society is not a mere coincidence: as Morris makes clear, the achievement of the latter is a direct consequence of the former. When discussing the absence of divorce disputes with an old man that he meets, William's enquiry meets with the following reproach: 'Well, then, property quarrels being no longer possible, what remains in these matters that a court of law could deal with?' (49). The same logic holds with the issue of crime. As the old man further explains, the majority of crimes 'were the result of the laws of private property, which forbade the satisfaction of their natural desires to all but a privileged few' (70). The abolition of property has thus dispensed with crime and removed the need for courts of law.

The end of private property also means that 'poverty is extinct' (56). Human needs are satisfied through the community working together in harmony. There is no culture of market exchange, as people simply take what they need when they wish to, and there are no wages necessary to reward labour, since the activity is not a chore, but a source of pleasure for those involved. During his narrative, Morris invokes a number of theoretical tropes of utopian socialism. One of them concerns the attractiveness of the freedom that individuals will experience under socialism. Morris's utopia echoes one of Marx's own rare speculations on a communist society, within which an individual can reject the specific 'sphere of activity' that secures her livelihood. For Marx,

> in communist society, where nobody has one exclusive sphere of activity but each can become accomplished in any branch that he wishes, society regulates the general production and thus makes it possible for me to do one thing today and another tomorrow, to hunt in the morning, to fish in the afternoon, rear cattle in the evening, criticise after dinner, just as I have a mind. (1972b: 160)

Such an emancipated way of living is detailed vividly by Morris in *News from Nowhere*: individuals live their lives by following the pastimes to which they are drawn and through which they find fulfilment. Like Marx, Morris sees the abolition of private property as something that enables freedom because the existence of property is part of an economic system that requires compulsion and drudgery.

What is perhaps most interesting in Morris's utopia is not his representation of the political and economic life of his imagined community, but the ethical lives of the individuals within it. His vision of communist society is one in which there is a demonstrable transformation in the values, priorities, and motivations of those that inhabit it. Egoism is something unseen, and kindness is the norm that governs interpersonal relations. His claim seems to be that, by definition, a world of *yours* and *mine* pits individuals against each other. As noted, it is to the existence of ownership rights – held selfishly against each other – that Morris ascribes responsibility for the antiquated need for law courts to adjudicate crimes or divorces and the need for government as a mechanism to overcome disagreements. The world without private property, by contrast, is one in which individuals align their own satisfaction with that of the community. 'It is', as one inhabitant puts it, 'a point of honour with us not to be self-centred' (Morris 2003: 50). Their interactions are instead characterised by good humour and laughter, and William's interlocutors greet even his relentless questions about their society – which after a while would surely be rather tiresome – warmly with an open, welcoming curiosity for the alien world beyond their own. It is, of course, exactly such idealised circumstances that make Morris's story so open to mockery by critics who are committed to either Hobbes's cynical conception of human nature (and the proneness to conflict it implies) or to a belief in the necessary scarcity of material resources. While neither of these two assumptions is perhaps uncontroversial in itself, each requires as much faith in a negative view of human nature (which the scarcity thesis implicitly relies on) as Morris invites us to have in his alternative. Morris's socialist vision is – to its credit and unlike the Hobbesian view – built on a recognition of the contingency of human institutions and the inherent malleability of individual behaviour. His depiction of a communist life might appear far-fetched, but it certainly gives us reason to pause and wonder what might justify private property, given everything we might hope to gain by its abolition.

Conclusion

This chapter has considered a very small selection of the most strident critics of private property. After examining their criticisms, we can hopefully now appreciate the political urgency of – as well as the intrinsic philosophical interest in – coming up with a compelling normative justification for its existence. There were several recurring themes in the arguments advanced by Rousseau and Proudhon. Each alleged that there was a connection between the existence of property and a regrettable level of inequality – both material *and* social – in political communities. Their worry was that political and legal apparatuses seemed intentionally designed to protect the rights of the proprietor class and so enabled and perpetuated material inequalities. For Proudhon, this inequality results in radically unequal power and influence in society. For Rousseau, such material inequalities result not only in political inequalities, but also in a social and cultural degradation experienced by the rich as well as the poor. Both Rousseau and Proudhon offered criticisms of property that were consequentialist on the one hand – pointing to the misery caused by private ownership as an institution – and those that invoked matters of independent moral wrongness on the other. They mocked what they saw as the eccentric premises or contradictory arguments at the heart of defences of ownership, and challenged the fictional pristineness of the historical narratives upon which those defences implicitly or explicitly relied.

Our discussion then turned to Morris's utopian vision of what life would look like without private property. Though his depiction of a socialist future is exactly the sort of thing that would fail to convince those committed to a Hobbesian view of human nature, its hopeful vision contains much profundity. Drawing on Rousseau's insight into the radical plasticity of human attitudes and behaviour, Morris's suggestion is that many of the darkest and most regrettable features of society, such as crime, poverty, jealousy, and domestic violence, are ultimately traceable to the sanctity of private ownership as an individual right. By suggesting that life without property removes conflict and selfishness, he is of course arguing that its existence is the ultimate *cause* of such vices in our own society. By positing an ethics of kindness and selflessness as an alternative, he invites us to take seriously a different way of thinking about our lives. Morris's narrative – as with the arguments of Rousseau and Proudhon – is not presented here as providing a knockdown argument against private property. Each is rather supposed to focus the mind and signal some important considerations for evaluating the forthcoming defences of property. The anarchist and socialist traditions offer vital critiques that must be answered; they suggest that if no compelling justification of property is forthcoming, then it must be necessary and possible to further imagine a world without it.

2
Libertarianism and the Natural Right to Property

In the previous chapter, I discussed some arresting socialist and anarchist challenges to the legitimacy of property ownership and concluded that it stands in need of justification as a social institution. These challenges – which questioned the justness of the origins of the institution, doubted the coherence of the defences made of it, and cited its existence as a cause of poverty and significant inequalities – invite us to consider a world without private ownership rights. They encourage an alternative way of organising our economic life, one that does not include the possibility of a hard, exclusive distinction between yours and mine. Such criticisms seem to put the burden of justification on defenders of property. Given the problems that are ascribed to the existence of ownership rights, as well as the highly dubious ways through which such rights do appear to have been acquired throughout history, should we be working towards its abolition or transformation, looking for ways of organising our economic lives that do not involve private property?

I turn now to consider the most strident philosophical response to, and rejection of, these objections to private property. In this and the following chapter, I will examine the view that ownership rights are not merely justifiable, but actually are so important that we should protect them *at all costs.* In this chapter, I will first discuss Robert Nozick's *Anarchy, State, and Utopia*, which contains the most philosophically interesting libertarian conception of property in modern political theory. I will focus, in particular, on the role that the ideas of freedom and self-ownership play in Nozick's argument. In the next chapter, I will go back further into the history of Western political thought to examine how the core concepts that characterise Nozick's libertarian defence of property have a distant ancestry in early-modern and modern Christian ideas of natural rights. These natural rights theories offer justifications of property ownership that defend individual entitlements against the state. We find these theories – advanced by both Roman Catholic and Protestant writers – embedded within a general philosophical account of the nature of the world, including a comprehensive, religious understanding of natural law. Within contemporary political theory, however, libertarians like Nozick have abandoned any appeal to a natural law framework. I aim to show how the structures of such libertarian theories of property have secularised and suggest that the abandonment of a theological framework raises some difficulties for their arguments about the sacredness of individual ownership rights. I will conclude that, despite its apparent attractiveness, libertarianism is incapable of sustaining the strong claim that property rights must be protected from non-consensual taxation.

The inviolability of property rights

One of libertarianism's most prominent philosophical advocates, Jan Narveson, suggests that the definitive feature of the libertarian intellectual tradition is the view 'that the only relevant consideration in political matters is individual liberty' (2001: 7). In his contribution to the 'Key Concepts' series of which this book is part, Eric Mack likewise claims that 'libertarianism is advocacy of liberty as the fundamental political norm' (2018: 1). Narveson, Mack, and others cast the state as the most significant threat to such liberty – or freedom, as the terms are interchangeable – because of the vastness of its potentially coercive power. The standard

Weberian understanding of the state defines it as the body that commands a monopoly of legitimate violence within a community. It is undeniable that, in most theoretical and practical understandings of the concept, the state holds firm and complete authority over the individual even if the power held is never actually deployed. Suspicion of this power drives the intuitive attraction of libertarianism. Narveson thus begins his work *The Libertarian Idea* with an imagined scenario in which agents of the state come to your house in the middle of the night and place you under arrest for any number of possible reasons – which, after all, they customarily possess the power to do.

For most people, there is something undeniably frightening about the possibility of an all-powerful, monolithic state apparatus policing our personal lives, invading our homes at will, and seeking to use its force to thwart the choices we wish to make about how to conduct our lives. Dystopian narratives of totalitarianism – such as, most famously, George Orwell's *Nineteen Eighty-Four* – gain their force from our deep fears of such possible scenarios. As we will see, however, libertarians tend to have a very specific fear about the state's interference in our *economic* lives and its coercive power over the individual's *property rights* in particular. It is no accident that one of the imagined motivations Narveson gives for the state knocking on your door to terrify you in the middle of the night is 'because you make more money than most people and don't want to give it to others that have less' (2001: 3). In other words, it is worries about the redistribution of a person's rightfully owned income, wealth, or holdings that animate the contemporary libertarian political agenda. In philosophical terms, the key claim associated with the libertarian tradition is that there is an intimate moral and conceptual connection between the preservation of individual property rights and the preservation of liberty. Adherents of this view regard any threat to private property – including the coercive redistribution of holdings through taxation – as the paramount threat to liberty, to be resisted as far as is possible.

Though it was published in 1974 – and therefore before the consolidation of neoliberal economics under Ronald Reagan and Margaret Thatcher, over whom it had no demonstrable influence – Robert Nozick's *Anarchy, State, and Utopia* remains the most philosophically potent and provocative articulation of a libertarian political theory.[1] Nozick defends what he calls a 'minimal state', the only legitimate function of which is the protection of rights and the enforcement of voluntarily agreed contracts. This limited view of the state correspondingly implies the illegitimacy of coercive taxation, which, he concludes, is equivalent to forced labour. One of the main intellectual targets for Nozick's theory is the social-democratic view that the state has a redistributive function as a matter of basic fairness. Advocates of this view assert that it is morally right that the state redistributes resources through taxation to limit economic inequalities between members of a society and/or to ensure that its poorest members have access to sufficient resources to enable a decent standard of living.

In plain terms, this redistribution works by channelling financial resources away from the wealthiest members of society and towards the poorest, along the precise lines Narveson fears. The practical entailment of such redistribution *is* that agents of the state will compel you (though not necessarily by coming to your home in the middle of the night) to comply with the law. Whether such redistribution of economic resources is politically controversial will depend on culture and context. It certainly seems to be the case that many Western liberal democracies – particularly in Europe – have long-standing cultural and political commitments to forms of redistributive taxation. In the UK, for example, the modern welfare state guarantees access to publicly funded education and healthcare, economic protection during unemployment, and other provisions for citizens regardless of their ability to pay for it. That the state funds these commitments through progressive taxation, whereby individuals and families pay a larger proportion of their earned income as it increases, likewise seems a broadly accepted principle in many liberal democracies.

It is important to stress that, for Narveson, under such circumstances the wealthier members of a society essentially *provide* the publicly funded resources to their poorer fellows through the taxation of income and wealth. As Benjamin Franklin's adage notes, along with death, there is a *certainty* about the nature of taxation. It is compulsory. One cannot choose to avoid it, even if one is unimpressed with, or disapproves of, the specific policies that the state chooses to fund using it. Taxation is, by definition, a coercive business. Coercion is, however, hardly unusual in itself, even in self-described liberal societies with constitutional guarantees that protect individual freedoms. To pick a banal example, traffic regulations on highways restrict the freedom of car drivers as well as pedestrians and yet – as a general phenomenon – we accept them as an uncontroversial feature of social life. It is hard to imagine a functioning legal system without at least some coercive rules. What, then, do libertarians like Narveson think is so uniquely loathsome about the coercion of taxation in particular? What, if anything, is the moral difference between a traffic restriction and an income tax bill? In his answer to this sort of question, Nozick goes further than merely observing the coercive nature of taxation. He claims that non-consensual taxation – of *any* sort – is a violation of our fundamental individual rights.

How does Nozick reach this conclusion? He does so through a brilliant thought experiment that involves a wildly popular and successful sports star. Nozick first asks us to select what we regard to be a fair distributive principle for an imaginary society and to call it D1. As he leaves it to us to select the principle, it can take any form whatsoever. We could choose, for instance, to distribute holdings *equally* to every person in the society or, alternatively, select a principle of *reward* for people that recognises either their hard work or the display of some other kind of virtuous behaviour. We could pick a *utilitarian* distributive principle that allocates goods to generate the highest aggregate happiness, or we might even opt for something quite random and whimsical, like a scheme that varies a person's holdings according to height or hair colour. Whatever the principle or scheme that determines the distribution, the relevant point is that you are to select whatever *you* regard as a fair starting point for the imagined society.

We then proceed from this original distribution that we have selected (D1) to Nozick's hypothetical scenario involving a sports star. While he picks a 1970s basketball hero, to adjust the scenario for additional contemporary resonance – as well as for monetary inflation – let us imagine that the Portuguese footballer Cristiano Ronaldo's contract at his current club is shortly about to expire. He has performed exceptionally well during the previous season and proved transformative of his team's fortunes, securing them trophies and plaudits galore. Due to his splendid performances, he is able to negotiate a lucrative new contract, which contains a special clause that has the potential to increase his earnings for the coming season significantly. This clause stipulates that the football club place a box outside the entrance to the stadium where the team plays. This box has Ronaldo's name on it and each spectator is invited to donate 1 euro to him directly, in addition to whatever they have paid for their match ticket. During the season, Ronaldo's performances are better than ever. Spectators turn up to see him week after week with enthusiasm, joyfully dropping 1 euro into his box to enjoy the spectacle of his skills. The season ends with the fans delighted, though something important has changed in the economic structure of society over the course of that season, as a direct result of their behaviour. The donation box scheme has meant that Ronaldo's holdings have increased by 2 million euro, while those of the spectators have correspondingly declined because of their weekly 1 euro transfer to him. He is much richer, and they are all poorer. We thus now have a new distributive scheme – with a significant new inequality in terms of economic holdings and the power that comes with them – which we can call D2.

Nozick's provocative claim is that it would be unjust for the state to subject any of Ronaldo's 2 million euro income to taxation. Doing so would, in fact, be 'on a par with forced labor' (Nozick 1974: 169) – a clear violation of his rights that is akin to enslavement. Nozick thinks that taxation of these earnings would be illegitimate regardless of its purpose: not only would it be wrong to use Ronaldo's taxed income to fund healthcare provisions for the poor, it would also be wrong to use it to restore the initial distribution that characterised D1. Such redistributive taxation would, for Nozick, amount to theft of Ronaldo's rightfully owned property. Why does Nozick think this? The answer appears at first to come down to the characteristic libertarian worry about the state infringing on *freedom* – in this case, both the freedom of Ronaldo himself *and* that of the spectators who opted to transfer their money to him. Nozick thinks that any intervention to redirect the economic holdings in question in such a way as to benefit a third party (regardless of the reasons for doing so) undermines the freedom of the parties to partake in a private financial transaction. As we will see, however, he seems to understand freedom ultimately in terms of inviolable property rights, a position that will create challenges for the coherence and sustainability of his libertarianism.

Property and freedom

As observed, libertarians claim to be interested primarily in freedom or liberty, and Nozick emphasises that this idea is at the heart of his case against taxation. The unequal distribution that has emerged with D2 – wherein Ronaldo holds much more money than the spectators – came about through the exercise of *free* choices on the part of the individuals involved. The spectators could, Nozick stresses, have *chosen* to spend their money in other ways: they could have used it to purchase bars of chocolate or put it aside to save for a holiday (1974: 161). But they did not choose to do so. These people made a deliberate and conscious choice to transfer their holdings to another person – they did so happily and without any coercion. The contract into which Ronaldo entered was likewise a matter of *voluntary* agreement with the club, a free choice for both parties. Every stage in the move from D1 to D2 involved the exercise of free choice.

The challenge issued by Nozick is therefore the following one: 'if D1 was a just distribution, and people voluntarily moved from it to D2, transferring parts of their shares they were given under D1 ... isn't D2 also just?' (1974: 161). Nozick's assumption is that you will agree with the force of this question and accept that D2 is, in fact, just. It was, after all, *you* who selected D1 as fair, and all that happened subsequently to alter this distributive allocation was a bunch of consensual transactions. To re-establish D1 through taxation sounds like an unwarranted interference not only with Ronaldo's freedom, but also everyone else's. It would ignore the fact that people have important reasons for transferring their ownership rights to others. Such transfers express our personalities and reveal our ethical priorities and moral values. We can opt to direct our holdings not only to our favourite sports stars, but also to political parties, or charitable causes. We can patronise our favourite bookshops and restaurants, or put an investment aside to support the education of our children. Nozick's claim is that taxation of the recipient of such transfers would imply the justification of *constant* state interference in the lives of individuals, thwarting their freedom of choice. His pointed conclusion is that with such a role the state essentially 'would have to forbid capitalist acts between consenting adults' (163). Redistributive taxation thus appears to have a kind of totalitarian force. Repulsion at this prospect – of agents of the state coming to Ronaldo's house in the middle of the night to take some of the money you *chose* to give him to watch him play football – accounts for the appeal of the fundamental libertarian hostility to taxation in the name of freedom.

The genius of Nozick's example lies in its simplicity and its strong intuitive purchase. For many people – including those with a principled moral commitment to the concept of redistribution – taxation really can *feel* like an unwelcome invasion of supposed property rights. In their theoretical analysis of tax policy in the United States, Liam Murphy and Thomas Nagel (2002) cast this phenomenon as an 'everyday libertarianism' that exists in the backs of citizens' minds when they consider their pay cheques. As they point out, while relatively few citizens express a hostility as strong as Nozick's towards all forms of taxation, there does still exist a much larger proportion who retain a kind of latent libertarian view of the very nature of income and taxation. For Murphy and Nagel, this view amounts to the 'idea that net income is what we are left with after the government has taken away some of what *really* belongs to us' (2002: 35). In other words, many often believe that they are fully entitled to their *pre-tax* income as a matter of moral right. This everyday libertarianism means that even if these people recognise the case for some legitimate taxation, their belief is that its rightness stems from the fact that *they would* have consented to it if given the opportunity. The idea is that such people look at their tax return, see the amount that has gone to the state, feel a pang of disquiet about that transfer, and then acknowledge its legitimacy through some kind of retrospective endorsement. The reasoning perhaps runs something like 'I can see how, were I expressly asked about it, I would consent to taxation to fund a police force to protect my rights, or a healthcare system to help the sick regardless of their ability to pay for it.' The idea lurking behind this perspective is the everyday libertarian view that people own *all* their income before it is subject to the tax to which they would have consented had they been asked.

To establish whether this feeling of *pre-tax ownership* is justifiable – and significant enough to defend a potentially inviolable entitlement to our holdings under all circumstances – we need to dig a little deeper into the logic of Nozick's theory and determine exactly which concepts are doing the hard work in his argument. G. A. Cohen (1995) advances a powerful and revealing critique of Nozick's libertarian theory through a sustained form of such digging. The part of Cohen's analysis most relevant to our discussion concerns how Nozick understands the concept of freedom and how this then links to his account of property rights. Cohen rehearses a familiar political conversation between libertarians and socialists (1995: 57). Within this conversation, libertarians defend capitalism because of the freedom it guarantees for all, and socialists respond by claiming that there is less freedom for poor people within that economic system. The rejoinder from the libertarian is that the socialist is guilty of a conceptual confusion and a misuse of language. For the libertarian, the poor do not lack *freedom* under capitalism (because they have exactly the same liberties as everyone else), but rather lack *resources*, and one cannot redistribute resources without threatening freedom. There is, so the classic political argument goes, a necessary economic balance of, or trade-off between, freedom and equality, and if you are committed to the former as the most important political value, then the libertarian case for unfettered capitalism should be compelling and the socialist complaint defeated.

In this political conversation, freedom is construed in conventional, *negative* terms, as a mere absence of physical interference, rather than in any more demanding way that might depart from our everyday understanding. As noted earlier, on the negative understanding of the concept, a person is free to the extent that they are unobstructed by another. A key aspect of this conception of freedom is that it is purely physical and therefore *non-moral* and unconnected to individual *desire*. On this understanding, a person is unfree when locked in a cell, regardless of whether they wish to leave it, and regardless of whether they are justly imprisoned.[2] Freedom is not a matter of right or wrong, but just of the possibilities for unobstructed physical action. Cohen's suggestion is that proper philosophical attention to this commonplace, negative understanding shows that the very existence of property as an institution regulates and therefore *impedes* freedom in exactly the same way that taxation does. The reason for this impediment is that, as noted in the introduction, the ownership of property customarily governs the rightful interactions of agents, most often by ascribing duties of non-interference to non-owners. In a society in which private property rights exist, I cannot simply take your car for a drive without your consent, and nor can you decide – even if you are homeless – to pitch a tent in my garden uninvited. In each case, the rights to ownership entail corresponding duties not to interfere with the owned object, which the police and relevant legal authorities, in turn, will enforce.

Such conventional private property rights thus inevitably involve a restriction of negative freedom – after all, if they did not, there would not be much point in having them. What does this apparent fact about the nature of property rights reveal? For Cohen, it demonstrates that there is no reason whatsoever to think that property rights promote or protect freedom any more than redistributive taxation does. When it comes to negative freedom, taxation certainly restricts it, because, as noted, it *compels* individuals to act in accordance with it. This restriction is, however, no different in nature from the way in which specific property rights restrict the freedom of everyone *except* the owner of the holding in question. On this understanding, *everyone* apart from Ronaldo is less free than they otherwise would be if the law protects and upholds his property rights. The libertarian may respond by saying that we must uphold Ronaldo's property rights because the freedom of proprietors is simply more important than the freedom of those excluded from ownership. We would need, however, some grounds for accepting such a claim. The grounds could obviously not refer to the special value of the freedom that ownership grants the proprietor, because this move would merely further emphasise how significant it is for the excluded to *lack* that freedom. Nor could the grounds relate to any notion of deservingness on the part of the proprietor. The whole point of the Ronaldo example is to show the value of individual choice in guiding the transactions made. As Nozick is so keen to point out – in his rejection of what he calls *patterned* principles that fix upon specific distributive arrangements – exercises of choice, by definition, do not track considerations of the meritorious status of the recipient. Such choices track only the wishes of the person making the transfer. It seems then that the libertarian defence of rights against taxation cannot be justified with reference merely to the specialness of the proprietor's freedom or their status as a deserving owner.

If this thesis about the connection between freedom and property is sound, then it evidently becomes a matter of contingent empirical calculation – rather than a matter of principle – as to whether redistributive taxation reduces or enhances freedom within a society (Cohen 1995: 54). In other words, if freedom is the paramount value, we need to work out which of the two institutions – private property *or* redistributive taxation – provides better protection for it. Cohen thinks that such a calculation will not be friendly to the libertarian account of property within a capitalist society. He argues that the function of money within a capitalist economy is essentially as a 'freedom-token' that enables certain actions for individuals, as it allows us to do things we want to do without interference from others. The implication of this is, of course, that a lack of such freedom-tokens physically *prohibits* certain actions for individuals, because those actions – whether buying clothes, going on holiday, or seeing Ronaldo play football – will require money. If they try to engage in such activities without the relevant property (money), the necessary authorities will then forcibly restrict them. There would therefore seem to be a strong freedom-based case *for* taxation. Indeed, perhaps spreading the freedom-tokens around society in an egalitarian manner would actually *liberate* citizens, enabling them to undertake actions that would otherwise be impossible. Cohen thus concludes that socialists can legitimately argue that disrupting and redistributing private property could, contra Nozick, *increase* freedom significantly under capitalism. Whether this conclusion is accepted or not, the main implication of Cohen's argument is that libertarians need urgently to supply an additional, compelling reason as to why the freedom that comes with the ownership of property is more important – and so worthier of protection – than the freedom that is restricted by its existence. A commitment to freedom cannot, it seems, itself be sufficient to uphold a right to private property that is inviolable to taxation.

The concept of self-ownership

Nozick has been criticised for offering a theory of 'libertarianism without foundations' (Nagel 1975). This allegation refers, in part, to his apparent reluctance to explain fully the *origins* of the rights that he postulates. What, then, might be the basis for Nozick's ascription of rights? We can perhaps understand the rights as being rooted in a commitment to the egalitarian idea – associated with the moral philosophy of Immanuel Kant – that we should treat individuals as ends in themselves rather than as means to ends. In other words, we should not promote moral rules or political institutions that regard individuals as instrumental to the achievement of a larger end. Utilitarian theories in moral and political philosophy – those characterised by the view that it is right to pursue the action or policy that generates the greatest happiness for the greatest number – notoriously fail to live up to this moral commitment. For the utilitarian, happiness is the end and everything else – including what we might think of as valuable individual rights and freedoms – is always considered a means to that end, and so vulnerable to sacrifice for that purpose. Since the latter half of the twentieth century, many philosophers have developed theories, in opposition to utilitarianism, that try to capture and express this Kantian moral idea of individuals as ends in themselves. Perhaps the best way to understand the libertarian case for self-ownership and the rights that come with it is as such an expression.

The claim that the foundations of libertarianism are ultimately Kantian – and that Nozick's ascription of inviolable rights represents a contestation of what counts as adequately treating individuals as ends rather than means – has some plausible textual basis in *Anarchy, State, and Utopia*. Nozick is clear that he intends his defence of the 'libertarian constraints' on permissible individual action to 'reflect the fact of our separate existences' (1974: 33). The problem that such a Kantian reading of Nozick faces is not its accuracy or fidelity to authorial intentions, but rather its philosophical power. While it does make sense to understand Nozick's ascription of individual rights as an instantiation of the fundamental Kantian commitment, it is unclear that his libertarianism is the most persuasive interpretation of the moral idea at issue. The abstract Kantian idea of treating people as ends rather than means has both the freedom and the equality of individuals at its heart. The attraction of its rejection of the ruthless utilitarianism that threatens rights is surely that *all* individuals are entitled to such protected treatment. As our discussion in the previous section indicates, however, it is not obvious why the libertarian commitment to inviolable property rights is more faithful to the idea than any redistributive alternative. We again need to know why the protection of Ronaldo's rights against state taxation would be more important than the rights of those thereby excluded from his property.[3] The libertarian response to this worry cannot be that Ronaldo has property rights while the spectators do not, because whether this is the case is exactly the question at issue.

Cohen offers an alternative interpretation of the philosophical underpinning of libertarianism, one that does not regard freedom as its definitive value. His solution is for Nozick and his fellow libertarians to concede that their case against the taxation of property cannot, in the end, actually be about freedom at all. As Cohen points out, the only way in which it could be about freedom would be if we conceived that concept not in the everyday way concerning physical interference, but instead defined it explicitly *in terms of* the violation of property rights. Such an alternative view would construe the meaning of unfreedom as the specific infringement of property rights. The huge problem with such an approach, however, is that it would render Nozick's entire argument hopelessly circular. The reason for the circularity is that the initially distinct non-moral and moral concepts would become identical. For Nozick's argument to hold together – for it to count *as* an argument rather than a mere assertion – the two concepts instead need to be different: he needs to be able to say that taxation is an injustice *because* it involves a morally unacceptable violation of freedom. And yet if he defines freedom in terms of a violation of property rights – which he has to do to be able to distinguish the wrongness of taxation from the rightness of upholding Ronaldo's inviolability to it – the two concepts (of freedom and justice) become equivalent and there is only circularity and therefore assertion rather than any derivation.[4]

We cannot define freedom in terms of the violation of property rights without abandoning our everyday understanding of the concept of freedom.[5] It would seem then that Nozick is unable to invoke freedom to justify the case against taxation. This does not mean that his whole argument for inviolable property rights must collapse, but it does mean that freedom cannot be doing the important justificatory work in support of Ronaldo's claims against the tax collector. If the libertarian rejection of coercive taxation is not rooted in a concern for individual freedom, what can it be rooted in? Cohen suggests that the fundamental moral principle that supports libertarianism is *self-ownership* rather than freedom. He describes a commitment to 'self-ownership' as the view that 'each person is the morally rightful owner of his own person and powers' and therefore each has a right 'to use those powers as he wishes, provided that he does not deploy them aggressively against others' (1995: 67). The self-ownership principle – that we have full ownership rights over our person – can explain both why it is illegitimate to tax Ronaldo's income and why the (self-owning, but otherwise property-less) poor who can sell their labour power in the marketplace are in no way wronged by their economic position and have no claim to redistributive state assistance. Endorsement of the principle can also make sense of simultaneously defending Ronaldo's holdings against the coercive threat of taxation and using the law to keep a homeless person out of his garden. If Nozick's argument is about self-ownership, then there is no contradiction in holding both positions, whereas looking at the same situation in terms of mere restrictions on freedom would look weirdly one-sided in Ronaldo's favour.

The self-ownership thesis closes the logical gaps in Nozick's argument. There are also textual clues that suggest Nozick is aware of the principle that buttresses his libertarianism, providing the core justificatory premise that critics had thought was lacking because it was not explicitly advertised. During his discussion of taxation, for example, he advances the following case:

> Seizing the results of someone's labor is equivalent to seizing hours from him and directing him to carry on various activities. If people force you to do certain work ... for a certain period of time, they decide what you are to do and what purposes your work is to serve apart from your decisions. This process whereby they take this decision from you makes them a *part-owner* of you; it gives them a property right in you. Just as having such partial control and power of decision, by right, over an animal or inanimate object would be to have a property right in it. (Nozick 1974: 172)

This passage appears to reveal how Nozick's libertarian theory coheres around one central idea. His moral objection to taxation seems not to rest on any infringement of freedom *per se*, but rather on its curtailment of one's self-ownership and the corresponding property one has over one's physical person: when the state confiscates the fruits of your labour, or interferes in a consensual transaction, it is violating your self-ownership rights.

The legacy of Locke

Anarchy, State, and Utopia begins with the declaration that 'individuals have rights, and there are things no person or group may do to them (without violating their rights)'

(Nozick 1974: ix). We now seem – with the help of Cohen's analysis – to have drilled down to the logic underpinning the libertarian case for these inviolable rights: the principle of self-ownership generates these rights. What, in turn, does the moral commitment to self-ownership *itself* rest on and why should we take it seriously as a premise? What gives it such appeal that it can be a fundamental moral value for political theorising? Is it an obviously worthwhile place from which to begin theorising about normative principles? Perhaps the appeal of self-ownership is self-evident. The idea of having complete control over our own lives and choices does seem undeniably attractive, especially for political cultures with established commitments to individual rights. The example of the hypothetical move from D1 to D2 ascribes moral sanctity to individual choices through appeal to the consensual nature of the transactions or contracts in question: the spectators *choose* to transfer their holdings to Ronaldo and, for Nozick, we should respect such choices. As we observed, people have all kinds of personal *reasons* for making specific property transfers that carry (and display) obvious ethical resonance. The relevant question is thus whether the moral value of choice is of such importance that it trumps our other, rival normative political commitments.

In our imagined society, one of Ronaldo's spectators may encounter misfortune and come to need expensive medical treatment to address a debilitating health condition. This condition might be serious enough to undermine the *value* of her self-ownership, by curtailing her ability to exert the labour power she possesses and reducing her capacity to make meaningful choices and take control over her life. She will continue to own herself, but this will be of little comfort to her if she cannot hire out her labour power for income and is therefore not able to afford healthcare to treat her condition. In such a scenario, her self-ownership has no meaningful power. Nozick does not consider such a possible outcome, but the logic of his libertarian argument would seem to be that the person in question must rely on a chari-table, voluntary transfer from another – perhaps Ronaldo himself, were he feeling generous – to afford the medical treatment. Such philanthropic donations may well be forth-coming; capitalist societies with low levels of taxation often boast impressive rates of charitable funding. However, there would be, by definition, no compulsion for such donations, which would therefore place the needy at significant risk. In Nozick's minimal state, there is certainly nothing to protect (ostensibly self-owning) individuals from this kind of misfortune. The fact that suffering and possible perishing is a potential consequence of the libertarian political system endorsed by Nozick and others pushes us to establish what could be so morally special about self-ownership as to allow these implications and thus override our other normative commitments.

Perhaps we can turn to the history of self-ownership to reveal its moral appeal and defend the libertarian conception of property as a right that is sacred and inviolable under all circumstances. The intellectual roots of self-ownership are usually traced to the political writing of late seventeenth-century philosopher John Locke, whose *Two Treatises of Government* (1689) contains one of the most important and influential attempts to justify property as a social institution.[6] Understanding the logic of Locke's argument – as well as its own philosophical foundations – is vital for a considered evaluation of Nozick's libertarianism as well as for any theory of property based on fundamental individual rights. The main target of Locke's *Two Treatises* is Sir Robert Filmer's *Patriarcha* (1680). In that work, Filmer (2008) offers his own account of property ownership. He claims that the royal right to claim ultimate ownership of *all* English property is absolute, having descended through a line of inheritance originating with God and Adam. No mere individual subject can claim a rival property right, because all things belong to the King. Locke delves into scripture in the *First Treatise* to show the logical contradictions and textual inconsistencies in Filmer's attempt to find theological authority for his patriarchal account and then defends his own, radically different viewpoint in the *Second Treatise*. Therein, Locke argues that individuals can (and, crucially, as we will see, *should*) come to acquire private property rights over the natural world. These rights must then be guaranteed protection against interference from the rest of the world, including any sovereign ruler who wishes to invade them.

Locke outlines his case for property against the background of a law of nature, which is an ahistorical moral standard against which all individuals and governments are bound. Some of its precepts have directly inspired libertarian commitments, most obviously Locke's claim that this law stipulates that 'no one ought to harm another in his Life, Health, Liberty, or Possessions' (1988: 271). Providing further grist for the Nozickean mill, in his discussion of the extent of legislative power, Locke notes that

> if any one shall claim a *Power to lay* and levy *Taxes* on the People, by his own Authority, and without such consent of the People, he thereby invades the *Fundamental Law of Property*, and subverts the end of Government. For what property have I in that which another may by right take, when he pleases to himself? (1988: 362)

Such sentiments appear to point to the invulnerability of property rights to state taxation. The starting point for Locke's theory of property is nevertheless a situation of original communism, a world in which God has given the Earth, not to Adam specifically, but rather to everyone *jointly* ('to Mankind in common') (1988: 286). The intellectual challenge that Locke sets himself is to show how this initial situation of communism was legitimately disrupted – through the creation of property rights – *without* securing the consent of others (286). He needs a theory that shows why property rights end up being held by individuals rather than either ultimately by the sovereign (as suggested by Filmer) *or* communally together (as Locke himself claims was God's original intention). This is a tricky theoretical path to navigate and Locke's attempt to do so has proved perennially riveting to political philosophers.

Chapter five of Locke's *Second Treatise* – 'of property' – contains some of the most important and influential passages in the history of Western political thought and merits careful reading. It is here that what appears to be a variant of the idea of self-ownership enables Locke to defend individual property rights against the rival demands of the sovereign and wider society. He begins by noting that although God gave the world to all in common, there still must be a means through which individuals can come 'to appropriate' portions of the natural world 'before they can be of any use' (1988: 286). Locke then explains that:

> Though the Earth, and all inferior Creatures be common to all Men, yet every Man has a *Property* in his own *Person*. This no Body has any Right to but himself. The *Labour* of his Body, and the *Work* of his Hands, we may say, are properly his. Whatsoever then he removes out of the State that Nature hath provided and left it in, he hath mixed his *Labour* with, and joyned to it something that is his own, and thereby makes it his *Property* ... For this *Labour* being the unquestionable Property of the Labourer, no Man but he can have a right to ... (1988: 287–8)

We can see the germ of the libertarian conception of property in this passage. Locke's suggestion is that individuals can come to acquire apparently *exclusive* property rights over parts of the world through the application of their labour, because they (and nobody else) *own* that labour themselves. If I use *my* hands (which I own) to tend a vineyard that comes then to yield grapes, it is, for Locke, obviously right that those grapes belong to me. He later makes clear that with this legitimate acquisition through labour come the other conventional rights that accompany ownership. For example, I can use the grapes that I own to make wine, which I then have, in turn, the right to possess and to use, as well as the power to transfer through gift or exchange.

Locke's justification for private ownership seems, at first glance, to be rooted in the principle of self-ownership. Individuals own their labour, and, through its investment in the natural world, property is established. Before we investigate his commitment to self-ownership any further, let us look at some of the other important details of his account of property. In the passage above, Locke specifies the means through which we acquire property. We *mix* the labour that we own with the natural world to generate exclusive rights. Locke refers to 'the Grass my Horse has bit' and 'the Ore I have digg'd' as being subject to legitimate appropriation provided there was no prior ownership right (1988: 289). It is important to stress that it is the *purposeful activity* of *labour-mixing* that establishes property rights. When a deer is hunted, it is not the person first able to get to the carcass that can claim a legitimate title to it, but rather the person who killed it (289).

The legitimate acquisition and ownership of property is, according to Locke, subject to certain conditions. The first is relevant after the appropriation of property and concerns the potential for spoilage. We can, thinks Locke, claim title to 'as much as any one can make use of to any advantage of life', but anything that is in danger of perishing before we can do so becomes more than our share and therefore 'belongs to others' (1988: 290). We cannot hoard our apples to the point of their spoiling, even if we first tended – and therefore came to own through labour – the tree from whence they fell. Locke's view is that this proviso does not apply to gold or money, on the basis that they are not at risk of spoilage and therefore we can accrue them without limitation. The second important condition on acquisition is relevant before property rights have even been established. It might be termed a *sufficiency* requirement, because it asserts that an individual act of acquisition is permissible only if there will remain afterwards an equivalent quantity and quality – 'enough, and as good' – of property left available for others. Legitimate ownership depends on the satisfaction of these two provisos. In apparent deference to Locke, Nozick offers his own version of this proviso within his libertarian theory, according to which initial acquisition is just so long as the position of everyone else is not 'thereby worsened' as a consequence (Nozick 1974: 178).

As long as these two conditions – concerning spoilage and sufficiency – are satisfied, private property acquisition is, for Locke, legitimate. He insists that 'as much Land as a Man Tills, Plants, Improves, Cultivates, and can use the Product of, so much is his Property' (1988: 290), and one of the main functions of political authority is to maintain and protect legitimate ownership rights. In his theory – which seems thus far to be proto-libertarian at least – property arises from initial acts of labour on an originally unowned world. This social institution comes into existence – this world of *yours* and *mine* – because of labour, but it is not yet clear why this purposeful activity is of such huge moral significance. As suggested, it might be explicable with reference to the idea of self-ownership, which is what does the important justificatory work in Nozick's theory, once his concern with freedom evaporates. In the next chapter, we will further explore the logic of Locke's argument to show how radically his worldview – and, consequently, his political philosophy – actually diverges from that of Nozick.

3
Natural Law and the Gnarled Roots of Self-Ownership

We have determined that self-ownership – rather than freedom – provides the crucial conceptual underpinning for Nozick's libertarianism. Furthermore, it seems that *any* defence of the absolute protection of property rights from state encroachments made in the name of freedom must end up relying on the principle of self-ownership. The reason for this conclusion is that only self-ownership can explain why the freedom of the proprietor has the moral significance (capable of justifying inviolable rights) that the unfreedom of the excluded lacks. The idea of self-ownership appears also to be prominent in Locke's account of property. Recall that Nozick presents the self-ownership principle unambiguously in terms of *rights*. It is our right to self-ownership that we hold against all other individuals (and relevant legal entities) and that the state must protect. Whenever an external agent intrudes upon your property without consent, as in the case of taxation, she violates this right of self-ownership. Upon first encounter – especially when seen through twenty-first-century eyes – Locke's political philosophy looks very similar to Nozick's, with its commitment to the fundamental importance of individual rights. For Locke, according to the eternal authority of natural law, 'no one ought to harm another in his Life, Health, Liberty, or Possessions' (1988:

271). Nozick himself appeals to the authority of Locke on several occasions. There are, however, enormous differences between the two theorists, and their points of divergence are crucial for an understanding and assessment of the libertarian conception of property as inviolable to interference through taxation.

As we have seen, in the midst of Locke's account of legitimate acquisition through labour, he asserts that 'every Man has a *Property* in his own *Person*' (1988: 287), a view that is venerated by contemporary libertarianism. It is nevertheless a mistake to interpret Locke's stated commitment as equivalent to self-ownership as understood by Nozick or any other modern, secular theories of individual rights. We are not *self-*owners for Locke. As Cohen points out, the self-ownership thesis endorsed by Nozick implies that 'each person possesses over himself, as a matter of moral right, all those rights that a slaveholder has over a complete chattel slave as a matter of legal right' (1995: 68). Self-ownership must have this meaning – that we have complete moral authority over our own bodies and actions – for libertarianism to have a clear and distinct political and philosophical identity. Nozick's libertarianism needs this commitment for his moral case against the taxation of property to make sense. Unlike for Nozick, however, for Locke we are assuredly not self-owners for the simple reason that we absolutely do *not* have the moral right to order our lives or determine our actions in whatever manner we see fit. For Locke, our moral lives are instead characterised chiefly by authoritative *obligations* that govern our conduct. These obligations are, in a meaningful sense, often owed to others in the form of respect for their individual rights, but their source is ultimately God. We are not self-owners for Locke, because *God owns us*: human beings have been 'sent into the World by his order and about his business, they are *his Property*' (1988: 271, emphasis added). An appreciation of this key, unambiguous, fundamental belief – that God owns us and that we are obliged to do His will – is crucial for understanding the structure of Locke's theory of property, how it fits with his whole political philosophy, and the consequent challenges for, and limitations of, modern libertarianism.

The role of theology in natural law theories of property

The substantial role that Locke's belief in God – and his corresponding account of His wishes – plays in his political theory is visible at the beginning of the *Second Treatise*. Here Locke offers a Christian affirmation of human moral equality and specifies the nature of the general duties that individuals have to their creator. In his description of the state of nature – human life without political society – Locke identifies a law of nature that is an eternal source of moral authority. It is not only eternal in that it stretches across time (and thus applies both outside of and during political society); it is also universal in that it binds *all* individuals and governments. We are, Locke suggests, the 'Workmanship of one Omnipotent, and infinitely wise Maker', and remain servants of that 'one Sovereign Master' (1988: 271). The fact that God created us means that we owe duties to Him. The most important duty we have concerns the preservation of human life – both our own (first and foremost) and the lives of others. For Locke, the 'Fundamental Law of Nature and Government' asserts 'that as much as may be, *all* the Members of the Society are to be *preserved*' and that the '*preservation of all*' is the ultimate '*end of Government*' (375). This duty of human preservation is as much a matter for individuals as it is for governments. Locke further elaborates on the personal obligations we face, when he writes that 'Every one as he is *bound to preserve himself*, and not to quit his Station wilfully; so by the like reason when his own Preservation comes not in competition, ought he, as much as he can, *to preserve the rest of Mankind*' (271).[1] In other words, we are not morally permitted (though we *are* physically able) to commit suicide and we are obliged to likewise act (*when* we are physically able) to ensure the continued existence of others.

Understanding certain texts in the history of political thought is often a matter of joining the philosophical dots to make sense of the arguments put forward. Taking seriously Locke's commitment to the moral duty of human preservation helps us to link up the ostensibly different arguments in the

Two Treatises and to explain the coherence of claims that might otherwise look peculiar when considered in isolation. This commitment is extremely important for getting a grip on his theory of property, and scholars who ignore it are likely to misunderstand his political thought completely. Locke's theoretical accounts of political and economic life do link to his moral beliefs. It is thus the fundamental duty to preserve human life that explains the legitimacy of the move from original communism to individual rights of exclusive ownership. Within our initial communistic situation, Locke thinks we have divine permission to establish permanent rights over parts of the earth through our labour. Crucially, the reason God permits us to act in this way is that doing so *secures* our preservation and promotes the preservation of humanity as a whole. In fact, Locke claims that while God initially gave the natural world in common for all, He did not merely *permit* us to establish property through our labour, He 'commanded' us to do so (1988: 291). The establishment of property through labour is *intended* by God, as he gave the world to human beings 'for their benefit, and the greatest Conveniences of Life they were capable to draw from it' (291). The acquisition of property thus embodies the fulfilment of God's wish that human life be preserved.

This *duty* of human preservation explains, in turn, the existence of the aforementioned provisos to Locke's account of legitimate acquisition. He insists that 'Nothing was made by God for Man to spoil and destroy' (290), allowing him to place a condition on ownership that would otherwise look out of place in a secular theory based on labour. After all, if it is purely my labour that grants me an inviolable title to the wine from my vineyard, why would I ever *not* be permitted to let it rot if I so wished? Once we recognise how property acquisition and ownership sustain human existence, it is no surprise that we are not allowed to let such provisions spoil, nor that we have a duty – when acquiring private holdings from the initially unowned earth – to leave sufficient resources available for others to make use of (through the 'enough, and as good' proviso). In fact, Locke thinks that the establishment of property through labour does more than guarantee our own preservation by giving us sustenance and shelter. He also believes that it helps further track divine intentions by securing the preservation of the human species through the improvement of the natural world itself. According to Locke, it is '*Labour* then which *puts the greatest part of Value upon Land*, without which it would scarcely be worth any thing' (298). Acts of individual labour, for him, seemingly benefit the whole community, even though property ownership also involves exclusion from what was once accessible by all. Locke thinks that it is reasonable to expect that there will be quite significant inequalities in terms of who owns property, and the divine command again renders these legitimate. According to him, although God gave the whole world to everyone, He nevertheless also 'gave it to the use of the Industrious and Rational' rather than those unwilling to use their labour, who should not benefit from the exertions of others (291).

We can see that labour is morally important for Locke because it enables us to fulfil our chief duty to our creator, which is to preserve human life. We will return to this issue through further engagement with Nozick, but let us first locate Locke's argument within a broader intellectual context to reveal the structure of natural rights theories and show how much they differ from modern libertarianism. Even though the *Two Treatises* is a text of huge significance in the history of thinking about property, it did not come out of nowhere. While it is a strikingly innovative work in many respects, it is also part of a lineage of influential natural law theories, within which ownership is also justified with reference to God and the nature of His will.[2] Early-modern Protestant writers such as Hugo Grotius and Samuel Pufendorf both justified the existence of private property within a natural law framework that, like Lockes, begins with a presumption of divinely willed original communism, the disruption of which was legitimate according to God's wishes. The iconic innovation of Locke's account of property is the central place that the morally praiseworthy act of labour has within it. Unlike Locke, Grotius and Pufendorf do *not* identify labour as the legitimate means of initial appropriation: the emergence of individualised ownership is, for them, not connected to the moral significance of the *act* of privatisation. Indeed, neither Grotius nor Pufendorf are particularly interested in exactly how property comes into existence or in the subsequent distribution of ownership rights. The important thing for them is simply that property as a social and legal institution *is* established. Their primary concern – which they identify as the central command of natural law – is the securement and maintenance of the peace that is required for self-preservation. Since the motivation for human conflict is, according to them, most likely to be rival claims for possession and use, the establishment of authoritative property rights is a basic requirement for (morally required) stability in political society.

For these political writers in the natural law tradition, the existence of private property rights is justified ultimately by our need to fulfil a religious duty, a compulsory obligation we owe to God. This tradition of embedding the existence of private ownership rights within a theological framework goes back further, to the Roman Catholicism of the Renaissance thinkers associated with the 'Salamanca School' (most notably Francisco di Vitoria and Francisco Suárez), which, in turn, found inspiration in the medieval Scholasticism of Thomas Aquinas. All of these theologically informed theories of property maintain that private ownership is justifiable only within a comprehensive account of natural law. Even where property is understood in such an account to be the product of human law, the demands of natural law inevitably act to regulate and limit its ownership. Aquinas is less absolute than his early-modern followers are when it comes to the necessary existence of private property. In the *Summa theologiae* (1485), Aquinas does not insist that we have a duty to establish private ownership. He does believe, however, that the institution is permitted by, and congruent with, the content of natural law. Furthermore, while his view is that the precise details of the 'division' of property are a matter for positive (human) law, natural law retains an important authority over its ownership within political society (Aquinas 2002: 208). We can see this authority in Aquinas' discussion of what constitutes theft. In the *Summa*, he articulates a proviso on legitimate ownership that would have an enormous influence on natural law theories throughout the medieval and early-modern period, as well as a key place in Roman Catholic thought for years to come. His claim is that instances of what would otherwise be theft are morally justifiable, and, in fact, perfectly 'lawful', when a person is in a state of desperate need. For Aquinas, although the private, exclusionary ownership of holdings is legitimate – being consistent with natural law – 'in cases of necessity *all* things are *common* property' (216, emphasis added). What this right of 'necessity' then means is that 'if a person is in immediate danger and no other help is available – anyone can then lawfully supply his own need from the property of another by taking from it either openly or in secret; nor, properly speaking, does this have the character of theft or robbery' (217). Aquinas is unequivocal that this right is a matter of legal justice, rather than merely personal morality, and therefore that the transfer of resources to the needy does not depend on the will of the relevant proprietor.

We find this commitment to a right of necessity in circumstances of desperate need articulated throughout later medieval and early-modern political thought, including that of Grotius and Pufendorf.[3] For Grotius, the justification for ownership is such that its intended distribution was 'to depart as little as possible from natural equity' (1925: 193). It therefore follows that 'in direst need the primitive right of user revives', such that 'if a man under stress of such necessity takes from the property of another what is necessary to preserve his own life, he does not commit a theft' (193). Similarly, for Pufendorf, if we find ourselves in desperate need then we can legitimately invade the property of another to preserve our life (1991: 53–5). For him, the permission of such invasions is a 'duty of humanity' (53).[4] In the political economy of the eighteenth century, this right of necessity transforms from an authoritative legal obligation into a voluntary moral obligation. For Adam Smith, for example, we do have such a duty to secure the sustenance of our needy fellows. It is, however, an *imperfect* duty that is morally binding, but not legally so, and can therefore be legitimately avoided (Smith 1978: 9). The distinction between perfect and imperfect duties is an easy one to grasp in modern liberal thought: we have perfect (legal) obligations of justice and imperfect (moral) obligations of charity. Though there is often lively debate about where the line between the two is drawn – as discussions about so-called Good Samaritan laws indicate – this itself reveals the vitality of the distinction. A desperately hungry beggar, according to Smith, can make demands on our property, but while we should assist that person, we *need not* do so, and he could *not* legitimately take our holdings without our consent. In modern liberalism, the duty to assist and the right of necessity are often uncoupled, such that they are not correlates of each other, as they are in natural law: for Grotius, Pufendorf, Locke, and others, the right of necessity implies an obligation of assistance even if this involves allowing the needy to invade our property.

Before the duty to assist becomes conceived as an imperfect (avoidable) obligation in the eighteenth century – and transformed into what we now understand as the liberal obligation of charity that is contrastable with that of justice – a version of the right of necessity is visible in Locke's *Two Treatises*. Though it goes unmentioned in the context of his discussion of property rights, Locke does offer one telling rehearsal of the view that natural law protects the welfare of those in need even when doing so compromises legitimate private property rights. In the *First Treatise*, again fending off the arguments of Filmer, Locke maintains that

> we know God hath not left one Man so to the Mercy of another, that he may starve him if he please: God the Lord and Father of all, has given no one of his Children such a Property ... but that he has given his needy Brother a Right to the Surplusage of his Goods; so that it cannot justly be denied him, when his pressing Wants call for it ... 'twould always be a Sin in any Man of Estate, to let his Brother perish for want of affording him Relief out of his Plenty ... and a Man can no more justly make use of another's necessity ... than he that has more strength can seize upon a weaker, master him to his Obedience, and with a Dagger at his Throat offer him Death or Slavery. (1988: 170)

The right of necessity appears here to be alive and well within Locke's understanding of political morality. It is again expressed in terms that underscore the overarching centrality of human preservation in his political theory: my needy brother has the right to my property (provided I have enough to survive myself), and failing to honour this entitlement is equivalent to killing him. For Locke – unlike for many modern liberals – there is no moral distinction to be made here between *killing* and *letting die* (or doing and allowing harm): the two are equivalent in situations of need. Although he describes the duty owed to the needy to be one of 'charity', Locke nevertheless insists that the property owner cannot *justly* withhold his surplus in cases where the preservation of another is at stake. While charity, to modern eyes, epitomises an imperfect duty, it has a binding status in Locke's early-modern Christian natural law framework, one that compels governments as much as individuals.[5] The implication of this argument, of course, as in the case of Aquinas, is that instances of what we would otherwise regard as theft become legitimate under circumstances of severe need.

Back to Nozick

Nozick does not invoke an explicit right of necessity that – when triggered by urgent need – would undermine the inviolability of private ownership rights. He instead incorporates a reinterpreted 'Lockean proviso' into his account of property. Nozick's version of the proviso does not mention spoilage, but it does try to take seriously Locke's commitment to sufficiency, through the insistence that a property right will not hold 'if the position of others no longer at liberty to use the thing [in question] is thereby worsened' (1974: 178). Although Nozick does not spell out in detail what a worsened position will look like, he plainly is committed to human preservation. His version of the proviso thus stipulates that a person cannot appropriate the only source of water available in a desert (180). While Nozick gets the inspiration for it from Locke, exactly how the proviso fits into the logic of his theory is unclear. There is no mention of natural law in *Anarchy, State, and Utopia*, except the observation that Locke's account of it in the *Two Treatises* is incomplete. Nozick suggests, perhaps reasonably, that political philosophy can proceed without a full account of the 'underlying basis' of a moral theory, as that task could take a 'lifetime' (9).

Were Nozick to have devoted more time to explaining the comprehensive moral basis for his libertarianism, it would evidently have been substantively different from the theological framework of Locke and the other early-modern philosophers who derive their political commitments from a divinely authoritative account of natural law.[6] It would be different because Nozick's rights-focused justification for property acquisition (based on self-ownership) is antithetical to the duty-focused justification found in Locke (where it is based on human preservation via labour) as well as Grotius and Pufendorf (where it is based on the need for peace and social order). There is no moral *end* to satisfy in Nozick's account of property ownership, as there is for these natural law theorists. The structure of his moral theory does not allow for it. The acquisition of holdings is certainly permissible in Nozick's modern libertarianism, but there is no reason to think it obligatory. If individuals do hold the far-reaching rights that Nozick thinks they have, this catalogue presumably includes the right *not* to hold property – beyond the ownership we have over our physical selves – which obviously means that they are under no duty to do so.

The reason that the focus on the *duty* (rather than just our right) to acquire property really matters for our earlier discussion is that it reveals both the historical novelty of contemporary libertarian political morality and the ultimate fragility of its philosophical foundations. These foundations buckle under the strain of defending the minimal state against the pressure of outrage implied by the prospect of the desperately needy being reliant on voluntary acts of personal charity. Nozick invokes Locke's authority but wholly secularises his theory. There is clearly no place in Nozick's libertarianism for any duties other than the general (negative) one to respect the rights of others. The standard libertarian attitude to moral conduct is that the right you have to your knife extends as far as you like but stops at my back, and my rights likewise can be invoked as long as their exercise does not cause harm to another (e.g. Narveson 2001; Mack 2018; Brennan and van der Vossen 2017). There is thus no conceptual room for any *positive* duties – no notion that we owe others anything in terms of our attention or behaviour, beyond non-interference with their rights – in Nozick's theory or in any form of contemporary libertarianism. The tradition cannot allow for such duties because they would pose a threat to our fundamental liberty to do whatever we like. Libertarians cannot make sense of any duties that do not exist to protect our rights not to have our bodies and property interfered with.

The crippling problem raised for libertarians by Locke's commitment to the moral priority of duties is not, however, merely that they cannot claim him as any kind of historical authority for their ideas. It is rather that without his framework, their central ideas lose their philosophical integrity and conceptual coherence and, correspondingly, their account of property begins to fall apart, as the principle of self-ownership emerges as a stark and arbitrary assertion rather than a compelling moral premise. We can explain this disintegration further through a return to the example of Ronaldo. Nozick describes his overall libertarian account of property as an 'entitlement theory'. He explains that it has three distinct parts: (1) justice in acquisition, (2) justice in transfer, and (3) justice in rectification. The example of Ronaldo's untaxable income illustrates (2). It is supposed to exemplify the fairness of allowing free transfers between individuals, and the corresponding injustice of a state interfering with them, thereby thwarting the self-ownership of both Ronaldo and his fans.

Much of the appeal of Nozick's argument – the main reason that we may feel an immediate intuitive pull in his direction – lies in the fact that he asks us to determine what D1 is. Doing so allows him to claim that because the starting point is fair (and it must be so because *you* picked it) and all that happens afterwards are consensual transactions, then D2 must also be perfectly fair. This reasoning might appear sound enough in a stylised thought experiment. What about, however, when we consider the real world, where the origins of established ownership rights are far less pristine than the unimpeachably fair handout of holdings that characterised D1? In particular, what about when we find that – as in the cases of post-colonial societies – established property was actually *stolen* from indigenous populations, insofar as they were forcibly removed from land that they occupied and used? In one sense, Nozick has no problem marshalling a response to this: such theft represents a wrong that must be righted. As is evident from the *rectification* element of his theory, Nozick thinks that justice requires the active correction of unjust holdings, something that will certainly require the confiscatory force of the state and a corresponding redistribution of holdings. For him, anything that fails to meet the standards of justice in acquisition or justice in transfer requires rectification. Given his ambition to offer a genuinely *historical* account of property, one that focuses on *how* things came to be owned – and not simply on 'who ends up with what' (1974: 154) – Nozick really needs to offer a compelling account of *justice in acquisition* for the idea of rectification to make sense. The example of Ronaldo illustrates a just transfer (and its potential thwarting), but we urgently need an explanation about how we can come to acquire property in the first place.

How, in the case of the thought experiment, can we be sure that the holdings given to Ronaldo have been *initially acquired* in a just manner? When he comes to explain the nature of a just acquisition, Nozick turns once again to Locke.[7] He raises some of the challenges posed by Locke's tricky idea of labour-mixing but, in doing so, ends up creating problems for his own theory. These problems make vivid exactly what happens to the libertarian conception of property when it loses the theological framework that it must abandon to retain its vision of inviolable rights based on self-ownership. In his sympathetic but critical discussion of Locke, Nozick asks the following set of questions:

> Why does mixing one's labor with something make one the owner of it? ... why isn't mixing what I own with what I don't a way of losing what I own rather than a way of gaining what I don't? If I own a can of tomato juice and spill it into the sea ... do I thereby come to own the sea, or have I foolishly dissipated my tomato juice? (1974: 75)

Nozick's worries here are twofold. On the one hand, there is the practical issue of exactly what it means to mix one's labour with something, but on the other, there is the more significant issue of *why* the investment of labour results in a gain of property rather than just the loss of labour. The relevant question therefore is *what is the moral significance of labour such that it justifies property rights (that are inviolable to redistributive taxation and to the claims of the desperately needy)*? As I have suggested, Locke has a clear response to this question about justifying the role of labour in his story about legitimate acquisition. Labour is a laudable activity because it *satisfies God's will* in its improvement of the world and sustainment of the human species. We have, in fact, a *duty* to labour – it has been 'commanded' of us – and a duty to preserve human life when it is possible for us to do so.

Nozick has no place for duties in his theory, and therefore really has no plausible means of explaining the moral significance of labour. He does gesture towards his own non-theological solution when he suggests that perhaps 'labouring on something improves it and makes it more valuable; and anyone is entitled to own a thing whose value he has created' (1974: 175). But this conclusion just moves the target of the justification at issue. It raises the question of why a person's entitlement would extend to the thing itself, rather than merely the value that she added to it through the labouring process. More pointedly, however, it would still not show the justificatory force of labour to be compelling, as it would not explain the value of the creative act in question. We still do not know *why* creating something is so morally significant enough to imply consequent rights of exclusion. We can certainly appreciate occasions where it might have such significance: if I use my labour to create a painting, it seems strange to think that it could ever belong to anyone else, even if it comes to hold huge aesthetic value to others. If, however, I use my labour to create something that can relieve the urgent needs of others – such as some kind of medicine – it is far less clear that I should have an inviolable ownership right over it. Nozick does, in fact, suggest that such urgent cases will involve a 'limit' to the kinds of property rights granted, which implies that the value of the creative act is not so important as to guarantee inviolable rights under all circumstances (181). Once we acknowledge such a limit, however, the general claims of the needy look much more potent, absent some notion as to why self-ownership generates the entitlement to acquire property through labour. Nozick's abandonment of Locke's theology gives contemporary libertarianism its distinct character through the idea of self-ownership and a civic life without perfect duties to others other than the observance of their rights not to be interfered with. Nevertheless, without the natural law framework that imbues labour with moral significance, this idea of self-ownership becomes something of a slogan, the enfeeblement of which is exposed whenever it encounters a more comprehensive normative call on our attention, as in the case of the desperate need of those without property.

Redistributive libertarianism

An exploration of the moral, rights-generating value of labour leads us towards other theorists within the libertarian tradition who have started with similar premises to Nozick but have reached very different political conclusions. Some of these writers have sought to combine the sanctity ascribed to rights of private ownership with a concern to *redistribute* property.[8] The whole idea of a redistributive libertarianism might appear oxymoronic, but it does capture a distinct, albeit minor, part of the tradition. One prominent libertarian argument for redistribution links to one of Nozick's questions about the value added to property through labour: that is, why does the private acquisition of property (if justified by an initial act of labour) imply an entitlement to the *whole* of the resource that is laboured upon, rather than only the *value added* to it through that act? This question does look tricky, even if we do assume that the creation of something establishes ownership rights over the newly existent resource. If I use my labour on a plot of land to cultivate a vineyard that yields grapes, why does my ownership stretch to include the original field (which I did not create) as well as the grapes and the vines (that I did), such that others are excluded from the *whole*? One potential response that the libertarian could reach for might be a utilitarian one. If we accept Locke's claim about the increased value of the natural world following acts of labour (1988: 296), then perhaps the libertarian could say that the ownership of the original land (as well as its products created through labour) is justified *on the basis* that it will secure overall improvement to the world. This argument is unconvincing though. It is unsatisfactory, in part, because of the lack of any meaningful conceptual relationship between the libertarian commitment to self-ownership and considerations of utility – since, as noted, key to the justification of self-ownership is a *rejection* of the aggregative consequentialism that characterises the utility principle. Perhaps more importantly, however, while Locke observes the increase in value that labour brings to the original world, his understanding of value is not detachable from his theological account of the law of nature, because it is deemed so on the basis that it fulfils God's wishes and not because it maximises utility.

It would assuage Nozick's worry if it were true that the physical mixing of labour with the natural world makes it impossible to separate the two, so that the exclusion that comes with property rights is simply unavoidable. If the separation of my newly created property (the value that I have added to the natural world) from the original property (the natural world itself) results in the destruction of my creation, perhaps we must accept that private ownership includes both elements. If the only way for my vines to continue to flourish is for me to own the soil underfoot then maybe I can justly claim an exclusive right over each. It may even be impossible to meaningfully *distinguish* the value that is actually added – in the case of a plot of land improved through agricultural cultivation – from any original value it held prior to that the investment of labour upon it. Perhaps, at least in cases of the natural world, the exclusive nature of private property is an inescapable product of labour as an effective, creative act.

The theoretical feasibility – and political urgency – of establishing the distinction between the original value of the natural world and the value added to it through labour is, however, exactly what the late eighteenth-century writer Thomas Paine proposes. In his work *Agrarian Justice* (1797), Paine makes the case for a significant redistribution of property that seems to imply a libertarian principle of self-ownership. In keeping with the natural law tradition, Paine believes that private property emerges from a situation of divinely willed original communism, wherein individuals were initially free to use the natural world in accordance with their needs. In parallel with Locke, for Paine, labour justifies the private property regime that has disrupted this communal ownership. Unlike Locke, however, Paine thinks that the creation of private property has not been a wholly positive development for commercial societies. For Paine, a previously unknown species of poverty has followed the establishment of private ownership and there is injustice as a result. According to him, a 'landed monopoly' has 'dispossessed more than half the inhabitants of every nation of their natural inheritance' and has 'created a species of poverty and wretchedness that did not exist before' (Paine 1969: 612). This analysis – which appears to mirror the concerns of later anarchist and socialist thinkers – prompts Paine to argue that while property ownership involves the recognition of legitimate rights for some, it has also *violated* the economic rights of others. He reaches this view by seemingly following a noticeably Nozickean argument through to a radically different political conclusion.

For Paine, the establishment of property as a social institution has been a random, contingent event, rather than the consequence of any command from God, whose only role in the economic life of His creation was to bequeath the world communally to all. There is therefore no moral duty to labour, and there is no requirement that we move from original communism to exclusive ownership rights. Paine's suggestion is that, at a certain moment in history, property became legitimately privatised through the deployment of labour on land. Although labour legitimately created such rights, he believes it has also violated those original rights that existed. How, then, to resolve the issue of the establishment of one legitimate right violating another? In *Agrarian Justice*, Paine offers the following normative assessment of the situation:

> the additional value made by cultivation, after the system was admitted, became the property of those who did it, or who inherited it from them, or who purchased it. It originally had no owner. While, therefore, I advocate the right, and interest myself in the hard case of all those who have been thrown out of their natural inheritance by the introduction of the system of landed property, I equally defend the right of the possessor to the part which is his. (1969: 612)

The ownership rights that Paine thinks legitimate were established by labour and are to be protected: individuals have legitimate claim to property in the form of the 'additional value' that was created through their labour. This claim means they own the vegetables they have grown but, importantly, not the field within which they grew. Such vegetables 'originally had no owner' and it therefore follows that they can only belong to the person responsible for their creation, who can only be the labourer. For Paine, the ownership right extends to the customary legal powers that come with ownership, such as bequest and transfer.

At the same time, however, those who were excluded – by the institution of private property rights – from the world that was once commonly owned must be guaranteed a right to their 'natural inheritance'. Paine's solution to this unjust exclusion is a redistribution through taxation. The object of redistribution cannot, he thinks, be the landed property itself and should instead be the *value* of the *original* portion of the natural world that is subject to redistribution. As it is not going to be physically possible for the original value to be separated from the added value, Paine thinks that the individual proprietor owes the community a 'ground-rent' that is to be collected through state taxation and appropriately redistributed in a manner that captures the egalitarianism of the original divine bequest. Befitting the libertarian aspects of his thought, Paine argues that the form that the required egalitarian distribution should take is a one-off universal financial endowment that allows individuals the freedom to pursue their own personal goals.[9]

With some help from Nozick's questioning about the logic of Locke's labour-mixing, we can appreciate why Paine's labour-based, libertarian justification of property acquisition can end up licensing a significant redistribution. This version of the theory appears to address some of the concerns about the plight of the desperately needy in a libertarian polity. Paine's redistributive libertarianism ensures that *everyone* is guaranteed at least the *value* of an equal share of the natural world in lieu of what he thinks is their inheritance. Other theorists have developed variants of redistributive libertarianism, with the aim of reconciling the principle of self-ownership with some kind of egalitarian conception of rights held over the natural world.[10] Some of these variants have provided interesting policy recommendations, such as a universal basic income that is supposed to secure meaningful freedom for all citizens by empowering them to choose how to use unconditionally allocated resources (Van Parijs 1995). Despite the inventive nature of many of these theories – both in terms of their philosophical creativity and their policy innovations – it remains hard to see how even the redistributive version of the libertarian theory of property can provide a compelling justification of private ownership. We saw earlier that if their theory is based on a commitment to individual freedom, libertarians cannot explain why the freedom of the property owner trumps that of the excluded or needy in such a way as to exclude taxation. We then saw that if their theory is instead based on self-ownership, the libertarian owes us an urgent account of the grounding for, and attractiveness of, that principle, given that it is ultimately detached from a more comprehensive moral framework committed to the sort of unavoidable duties that a minimal state could never countenance. Although the redistributive versions of libertarianism might illustrate how the problems of severe poverty and inequality are addressable while retaining the presuppositions that characterises this tradition, they fail to explain why we should endorse those presuppositions in the first place. In other words, we seem not to have any compelling reason to begin our political theorising from an assumption of self-ownership. Worries about nocturnal visitations from the officers of the law cannot themselves sustain a compelling libertarian account of property that renders taxation illegitimate.

There seem to remain two possible moves available to the libertarian in response to these serious objections to their worldview. The first is to advance a milder conception of self-ownership to buttress their normative theory. The second is to defend their political theories without any reference to the idea of self-ownership at all. The prospects for both of these moves appear bleak, however, insofar as neither will enable them to justify property rights that are inviolable to taxation and, if they surrender this commitment for something less absolute, the theory then seems to dissolve into a rather vague consequentialism. Making the first move, some advocates have suggested that libertarianism need not rely on Cohen's description of the self-ownership thesis as implying such an absolute and far-reaching account of rights held against the world. They think that libertarians can instead invoke a milder, markedly less controversial understanding of the idea of self-ownership, such that it means simply that each person 'has a right to live their own life as they see fit, consistent with the same right for others' (Brennan and van der Vossen 2017: 199). Self-ownership thus looks like the sort of principle anyone committed to freedom or equality can get behind, as it is simply the recognition of a set of individual rights against coercion. The problem with this move is that it purchases an increase in potential plausibility at the cost of normative distinctness. The blandness of such a refashioned vision of self-ownership means that libertarianism avoids the controversial implications of the strong (Nozick/Cohen) version, but this is simply because it has very few implications *at all*, beyond an unspecific commitment to an anaemic form of liberalism characterised by the existence of individual rights construed in terms of property. It gives us no reason to think of property rights as especially important (when adjudicating between the claims of someone with and someone without property), nor to be suspicious of redistributive taxation aimed at the promotion of other rights. Nor does it give us any reason to think of the rights we hold in terms of 'ownership' in the first place.[11]

Parallel difficulties bedevil efforts to make the second move and defend a Nozickean libertarianism by substituting self-ownership with some kind of end-driven, consequentialist justification for the minimal state. Versions of such a justification could involve a perfectionist idea of human flourishing connected to the ownership of property or a more general claim about the tendency of the minimal state to promote desirable consequences for society. It is undoubtedly possible to put forward a defence of property rights on such bases, though each appears to run aground quite quickly. In the case of human flourishing, it might plausibly be argued that private property allows individuals to achieve a certain end, or goal. We would still need to know why the flourishing of some (the property owners) would trump the flourishing of others (those without property), since, as noted, being without property is a possible entailment of the minimal state. A consequentialist justification for the minimal state could instead point to a broader sense of the desirable end achieved, such as, say, the economic growth or well-being of a community. The consequentialist argument for a minimal state will potentially attract some and repel others. Much depends on the consequence in question, which is where the problem for this justification lies. In pluralistic societies, it is reasonable to expect significant disagreement about the consequences we wish to see when we design social institutions and public policies. There is therefore no straightforward or uncontroversial way to define the success of a minimal state: any such measure will depend on prior normative commitments. Furthermore, the consequentialist nature of the argument also means that one's commitment to a minimal state will not be a matter of principle, but will rather be entirely contingent on the maintenance of (changeable) empirical connections between that economic arrangement and the nominated consequence. We therefore need assurance as to not only why we should prioritise economic growth (or whatever the preferred outcome is), but also a belief in its *necessary* connection to the minimal state, in order to sustain a definite commitment to libertarianism. We could give up on the *definite* nature of the commitment – and so allow the state to become *less* minimal under certain circumstances – but this would mean that normative questions of property ownership become matters of consequentialist measure, rather than of moral principle. We may have to settle for such a philosophically unsatisfactory outcome, of course, but we may also be able to do better.

Conclusion

Over the last two chapters, we have unpacked the logic of the libertarian defence of private property and corresponding rejection of taxation, with a specific focus on Nozick's political theory. For him, taxation violates the natural rights of individuals because of its coercive nature and, correspondingly, respect for property implies an absence of the confiscatory (and redistributive) reach of the state. The libertarian claim is that we are freer the more our lives

– and our holdings – are untouched by others. Nevertheless, while libertarians couch their political arguments in terms of freedom, I suggested that Cohen's interpretation of Nozick's libertarian theory is an accurate one and that a concern with this value does not do the work Nozick claims for it in his rejection of taxation. Nozick instead must be committed to a primary value other than freedom: that of *self-ownership*, which implies that taxation is wrong because it violates our right to absolute property over our own person, our labour power, and the individual choices over which we are sovereign. This reading of Nozick is the only one that allows his theory to hang together. My suggestion has been that the Nozickean conception of self-ownership cannot bear the weight that it needs to defend inviolable property rights when faced with the moral outrage prompted by their implications. While certainly not without intuitive purchase – especially within individualistic political cultures – libertarianism fails to explain why a commitment to self-ownership is of such moral importance as to justify the significant poverty and inequality that the minimal state can accommodate.

Locke's political theory does not face the same challenges as modern libertarianism because he is explicit that the very purpose of property as an institution is actually the preservation of life. Although he is committed to individual rights, his overall normative framework is a world away from modern secular individualism. Locke's theology thus actually enables his robust *rejection* of the idea of self-ownership as deployed by Nozick and others, since it involves substantial obligations to others that go far beyond a principle of non-interference, and explains the moral importance of labour in a way that modern libertarians cannot. As one prominent scholar of the tradition has recently suggested, 'libertarianism is … inconsistent with the justice, even approximate justice, of the modern state' (Vallentyne 2018: 110). The challenge for defenders of the natural right to private property is to explain not only why their theory is out of step with the modern liberal democratic state, but also why it departs so radically from the historical tradition from which it claims inspiration.

4

Property for the Greater Good: Utilitarian Theories of Ownership

It is not surprising that those seeking a compelling defence of private property are attracted to the natural rights that we find in the libertarian tradition of political thought. After all, private property involves rights held against others – without which there would be no *privacy* to ownership – and libertarian political theories are characterised by a commitment to the existence of such fundamental, inviolable rights. It seems intuitive to seek the justification for a right within an intellectual tradition that takes rights seriously. As we have seen, for a libertarian natural rights theorist like Nozick, individual rights exist regardless of whether political society does: the existence of such rights would seem to be a *natural* fact about the world that obtains whether humans choose to recognise it or not. Despite their divergent views of the sources and implications of such rights, Locke and Nozick share the belief that the fact individuals have them does not depend on their acknowledgement by others or the state. Indeed, any political society or government is, according to such thinkers, limited in its authority precisely because of these individual rights. The history of modern political thought is, however, replete with theories of property that do *not* appeal to such rights, and it is to such arguments that I turn in this chapter and the following one. In this chapter, I discuss three distinctly *utilitarian* approaches to property that seek to explain the value of private ownership without reference to rights as natural properties and instead justify its existence with reference to the good things it accomplishes or the ends it serves.

Utilitarianism as normative political theory

It might seem strange to look for a compelling justification of property rights from within the utilitarian tradition. The key utilitarian maxim, propounded by its originator Jeremy Bentham, was 'the greatest happiness for the greatest number'. Happiness is the only relevant end for the utilitarian, and all laws, policies, and rules within a political society should be formulated with the promotion of that end in mind. The legitimacy of any moral or political tradition or practice is thus automatically vulnerable on this basis. Utilitarianism came into being – in the late eighteenth and early nineteenth centuries – in explicit opposition to the idea of natural rights, a notion that Bentham famously derided as nothing more than 'nonsense upon stilts'. As an intellectual tradition, it is characterised by a scepticism about the trumping normative force of *any* individual rights, which would surely include the right to private property. Its definitive moral and political commitment – the utility principle – is consequentialist in focus, and so places intrinsic value only on the justice of future arrangements rather than those of the past. The grounds for, and character of, ownership might thus conceivably be quite different from the natural rights theories we have considered so far. There would, for example, appear to be no particular utilitarian interest in the question of what makes an initial acquisition legitimate. The utility principle has no necessary evaluative interest in questions of *how* things come about, but – to recall Nozick's terminology – is instead concerned with whether the distributive *pattern* of ownership serves to promote, or maximise, utility. If a proprietor's ownership of specific holdings does not assist the aggregate happiness of her political community, her rights over them then look vulnerable to legitimate utilitarian interference.

Despite this theoretical hostility towards the inviolability of ownership, utilitarian theories have historically proved quite friendly towards the idea of private property rights. Even though a concern with overall or aggregate happiness appears conceptually inimical to any sanctity ascribed to rights, the framework of the theory actually leaves plenty of practical space not merely to accommodate but to *prioritise* such rights. The result is that utilitarian writers have tended overwhelmingly to defend the institution of private property. The reason a utilitarian theory can prioritise rights is because of a supposed connection between their protection and the creation and securement of happiness and/or the greater good. If the utilitarian is interested in promoting happiness – however it be calculated – within a society, and if the existence of specific rights is demonstrably capable of guaranteeing that happiness, then it follows that the utilitarian must endorse such rights. This kind of rights-protecting, rule-based version of the doctrine forms the standard utilitarian rebuttal to various repugnant scenarios put forward by sceptical philosophers, such as worries about the permissibility of slavery, or the justification of one person's torture in the name of the greater good. A common utilitarian response to these scenarios is to insist that their acceptability is, in empirical terms, impossible because of the widespread unhappiness they would certainly cause. Thus, although utilitarianism, in its rawest form, is characterised by a hostility to rights, the tradition does have a quite straightforward means to justify their protection. It is important to stress that once they are justified, such rights have exactly the same robust form as they would for libertarians. The utilitarian simply explains their existence quite differently.

That utilitarianism tends to favour the existence of property rights is perhaps not so surprising when one acknowledges its fundamental individualism. Even though the utility principle, in calling for the greatest happiness for the greatest number, is an *aggregative* doctrine, at the foundational level it takes the *equality* of the individual persons involved in its calculations very seriously. 'Everybody to count for one, nobody for more than one' was the individualist and egalitarian mantra attributed to Bentham by his utilitarian follower, John Stuart Mill. Utilitarianism is rooted in a clear commitment to the moral sanctity of the individual, even if its ethical and political manifestations are often criticised for failing to guarantee her rights. When it first emerged as a systematic theory in the early nineteenth century, utilitarianism was not just a set of ideas discussed among scholars; it provided a blueprint for far-reaching social and political reforms, and the sweeping away of all traditions, practices, and institutions that failed the Benthamite test of aggregate happiness. Many of the proposed reforms were rooted in a commitment to individualism. It is not surprising that J. S. Mill – probably the most influential utilitarian philosopher – wrote his best-known work, *On Liberty*, as a defence of individual freedom against the social and political forces of conformity.

Hume and the emergence of property

Before we even get to Bentham's defence of property, we can consider the account of ownership advanced earlier in the eighteenth century, in David Hume's *A Treatise of Human Nature* (1739). Whether Hume counts as a true utilitarian is a matter of scholarly debate – as he was writing before Bentham elaborated his theory systematically – but his account of property is at least clearly *consequentialist* in nature, and the idea of usefulness is the key evaluative measure he invokes for questions of normative justification.[1] Hume explains and justifies the existence of property as a social institution with reference to the *ends* it serves, rather than basing it on any ascription of natural rights, an argument that obviously overlaps with utilitarianism. In his later works, moreover, Hume would develop an account of morality that is rooted in the value of 'utility', so there are clear links with the theory eventually articulated by Bentham.

Hume's account of property derives from the broader theory of justice that he outlines in the *Treatise*. Justice is, for Hume, an 'artificial' virtue, by which he means that it is not a sentiment that humans possess naturally. Our moral dispositions are instead necessarily partial, and directed towards those to whom we are closest, in various senses of proximity. We are, on this understanding, bound to feel a sense of moral obligation to our family, to our friends, and to those we regard as our fellows, rather than to any cosmopolitan impartiality. There is, for Hume, 'no such passion in human minds, as the love of mankind, merely as such', and 'our sense of justice and injustice is not deriv'd from nature, but arises artificially, tho' necessarily from education, and human conventions' (1978: 481, 483). The establishment of property rights is central to Hume's overarching narrative about morality and justice. His claim is that we can make sense of the emergence of morality as a social force through the idea of conventions. For him, it is evident that members of society have established a convention that has secured 'stability on the possession of external goods' and left 'every one in the peaceable enjoyment of what he may acquire by his fortune and industry' (489). The establishment of property rights – both in terms of settling the stable ownership of goods and the conventions by which they come subsequently to be acquired and to be transferred in the future – has effectively harnessed the self-interest of individuals to the overall well-being of society. It has created a situation where it is rational and to everyone's benefit to respect private property as an institution and therefore acknowledge the individual ownership rights that are recognised by law: for Hume, 'it will be for my interest to leave another in the possession of his goods, *provided* he will act in the same manner with me' (490).

Hume grounds property rights here not on a specific promise between individuals, but rather on a systematic scheme of social convention, one that has emerged gradually over time and not without practical difficulties. In fact, for him, we cement our commitment to property through the problems we observe in transgressions of its private ownership. We observe, for example, the disadvantages of the insecurity and even violence caused by instances of theft and, consequently, become more attached to ownership as an institution and more determined to protect rights over holdings (Hume 1978: 490). The very emergence of property as an institution corresponds with the development of justice as an idea in the minds of individuals. For Hume, the successful establishment of property tracks the success of moral sentiment in general, as the two are mutually dependent and reinforcing. Property is thus a vital part of the glue that holds political society together. This account of the justification of ownership rights then informs Hume's description of the rules and conventions that accompany its acquisition and transfer. It is, he thinks, crucial that the rules concerning property be intuitive, and not too 'abstruse', so that they are graspable easily by all and – as with other moral staples – communicable to children from a young age (493). Conventions surrounding the idea of ownership also specify its appropriate limitations. There are, for Hume, contexts in which relations of property have no place: he remarks that affection 'renders all things common among friends' and that within a marriage, there should be no notion of '*mine* and *thine*' (495). This view of the limitations of ownership for intimate relationships follows from Hume's account of property as a force for creating and sustaining moral obligations that he thinks we do *not* feel towards strangers. In the contexts of friends and family, there is no problem of scarcity or economic rivalry, and so the need for relations of property – and of rights/duties in general – does not exist.

For parallel reasons, there are certain objects to which the category of ownership would be inappropriate, such as air or water. Ownership is inappropriate for these objects not because they could not, in principle, be possessed by someone, nor because they are unimportant. It is rather because resources like air and water are not, in Hume's view, scarce and therefore no question of their *exclusion* or *distribution* arises. It is a combination of the scarcity of specific things and of the tendency of individuals to be selfish and partially interested that generates both the need for an accepted standard of justice and its subsequent invention. On this understanding, justice is – as Hume regularly points out – a concept that is characterised and justified by its *usefulness*. If it ever proved to be useless, he claims, we would get rid of it (1978: 496). Justice is grounded in the 'publick interest'.

Given that we have already observed the tight connection between the ideas of justice and property, it is no surprise to find a utilitarian account of the core features of ownership – likewise defended with reference to their usefulness – in the

Treatise. 'Property', Hume suggests, 'must be stable, and must be fix'd by general rules' (497). The nature of these rules – and their justification – is utilitarian. Hume thinks that, when society first emerges, private and exclusive ownership of resources is necessary purely for mere stability. It serves the basic purpose of *preventing* conflict. He is, however, confident that there will be no utility in maintaining this crude understanding of the purpose served by property beyond the infancy of that society. Such a basic understanding of the conflict-preventing purpose of property will, in fact, be 'pernicious', because it will not capture the complicated social phenomena that forms of ownership are able to protect and sustain. In other words, property has social benefits in addition to the prevention of conflict and, for Hume, it is vital that these benefits are widely publicised through established norms and so *acknowledged* as such within society. This insight about the need to publicise the benefits of property then has further implications for what he regards as the appropriate distributive rules for ownership. These rules depart from any primitive commitment to rights based on first possession. Since property fulfils many different functions in terms of its social usefulness, it will not always matter, for instance, whether the titles held over specific holdings are necessarily traceable back to the original possessor (Hume 1978: 508). While possession is likely the key way to identify ownership before we properly establish society, there are myriad subsequent ways to acquire property, including inheritance (509).

The 'right of succession' (or right to inherit) identified by Hume is an instructive example of how he uses utilitarian arguments to explain both the existence and value of specific traditions of property ownership. The tradition of inheritance, which establishes that possessions can be bequeathed upon death to those 'who are dearest' to the owner, derives, for him, not primarily from the consent of the relevant testator through a will, but from due assessment of 'the general interest of mankind' (Hume 1978: 510). It suits this general interest both to honour the wishes of the owner – whose stewardship will be rendered more responsible by the knowledge that the posthumous desires will be satisfied – and also to render their successors 'more industrious and frugal' in their conduct and attitudes (511). The thought is that the anticipation of an inheritance will encourage the recipients to behave more virtuously both before the posthumous transfer (to merit it in the eyes of the testator) and after (in respect of the value of the tradition which they will maintain through their own legal arrangements). We can see how Hume's utilitarian explanation of the emergence of property ends up providing a justification of private ownership as a social institution. His utilitarian approach to politics is essentially retrospective in its evaluation, but consequentialist in its prescription: it considers various moral and political traditions and institutions and explains their existence through reference to their revealed usefulness. As we have seen, Hume thinks that property emerges along with morality, but both become increasingly sophisticated in the ways that they serve complicated human interests after society is established. In the case of inheritance, a practice that begins as a legal way of instantiating the imaginative connection felt between parents and children ends up being justifiable in consequentialist terms, since its key social effect is to encourage individuals to behave in virtuous ways that are useful for the whole community. Hume's approach also provides a framework for justifying the appropriate taxation of property. For him – unsurprisingly, given his rejection of natural rights – the entitlement that one has over a particular holding is subject to appropriate levels of interference, justified with reference to the same social values (of usefulness and expediency) that explain the existence of ownership in the first place.

The utilitarianisms of Jeremy Bentham and John Stuart Mill

Bentham discusses property as part of his account of the 'principles of a civil code' within his overall theory of legislation.[2] Like Hume, he is keen to reject any notion that there exists a natural right to property. Instead, for Bentham, the existence of property rights – which he defines as 'the expectation of deriving certain advantages from a thing which we are said to possess, in consequence of the relation in which we stand towards it' (2001: 334) – is something that makes sense only as a social phenomenon and can be guaranteed only through law. Even the most primitive property regime based on a principle of mere possession, for him, comprises a law of sorts, with implicit rights and corresponding duties. Whereas for Hume the emergence of property coincides with that of morality, according to Bentham it is 'property and law' that 'are born together, and die together' (335). Bentham describes the expectation of advantage that defines property as 'security'. This idea of security – which 'consists in receiving no check, no shock, no derangement to the expectation' of ownership – is 'essential to the happiness of society' (335).

Bentham is quite convinced that property has made *everyone* happier. He offers a direct response to the sorts of criticisms we looked at in the first chapter about the poverty and misery that anarchists and socialists causally ascribe to the institution of private ownership. Bentham argues that the 'savage', pre-legal state ('the primitive condition of the human race') is where there existed genuine poverty (336). He offers the following diagnosis of the economic conditions experienced in modern society:

> The poor man, in civilized society, obtains nothing, I admit, except by painful labour; but, in the natural state, can he obtain anything except by the sweat of his brow? Has not the chase its fatigues, fishing its dangers, and war its uncertainties? And if man seems to love this adventurous life; if he has an instinct warm for this kind of perils ... must we thence conclude that he is happier than our cultivators? No. Their labour is more uniform [in civilized society], but their reward is more sure; the woman's lot is far more agreeable; childhood and old age have more resources; the species multiplies in a proportion a thousand times greater, – and that alone suffices to show on which side is the superiority of happiness. (2001: 336)

There is no equivocation here. Bentham is adamant that the unhappiness experienced by the poor in modern societies is trivial compared to the harshness of the conditions experienced in the natural state. Civilised society contains poverty, but those who experience it have (contra Rousseau, Paine, and other critics of commercial modernity) a far easier time than they would in the primitive alternative.

Property rights are, for Bentham, inextricably linked to happiness and human progress. Not only do private ownership rights make people happier by improving their material well-being, but – echoing the sentiments expressed by Hume regarding inheritance – their existence helps cultivate forms of virtuous behaviour that benefit the general good. For Bentham, property rights are key to the happiness of society as a whole because their existence discourages *idleness*. Much of his defence of private ownership hinges on its role in the battle against human laziness, which he regards as an especially dangerous vice. The ownership of property thus functions as a vital motivational force for both rich and poor: this enemy of our indolence has 'vanquished the natural aversion to labour ... given to man the empire of the earth ... has brought to an end the migratory life of nations ... has produced the love of country and a regard for posterity' (Bentham 2001: 337). The very fact that the existence of private property has the effect of discouraging laziness makes it, for Bentham, 'the noblest triumph of humanity over itself' (337). There is evidently no doubt in his mind about the huge value of a world of yours and mine.

There is an undeniably egalitarian element to utilitarianism as a moral and political theory, which connects to its fundamental individualism. Throughout his writings, Bentham shows a real concern about the evils of specific inequalities. His egalitarian instincts have, however, no significant redistributive implications in his account of property ownership. Bentham is quite adamant that the security ensured through the institution of ownership is far more important than any concern with reducing the material inequalities that it might tend to create. For him, a primary concern with equality in the economic sphere would pose a real threat to social cohesion and human happiness. 'When security and equality are in conflict', he suggests, 'it will not do to hesitate a moment. Equality must yield' (2001: 343). Security, he explains further, 'is the foundation of life; subsistence, abundance, happiness, everything depends upon it' (343). Bentham suggests that there are different distributive arrangements for private ownership rights visible throughout the world, but they are *all* far preferable to any alternative community of shared goods. One of his abiding worries about societies in which there is no private ownership is their tendency towards 'prodigality', with no incentive towards 'industry' (344).

In addition to the idea of incentives to work – again motivated by his fear of habitual human laziness – another key idea doing important work in Bentham's theory is that of 'expectations'. One of the main functions of the law is to create expectations for the individuals who are subject to it, and who therefore benefit from the happiness involved in holding those expectations: we derive utility from the knowledge that others will honour their contracts with us, that the state will protect our entitlements and security, and so on. In a world without natural rights, we need the security that our expectations will be assured. Expectations are themselves therefore an important source of pleasure and, more significantly, their assurance protects the happiness we anticipate in the securement of our various projects and commitments. Property nurtures expectations in terms not only of the pleasures of exclusive rights over holdings in the present, but also in the case of our *future* arrangements through the guarantee of posthumous transfers that reflect our wishes. I thus have an expectation that the law will ensure that my wishes as a testator are respected, while those who stand to inherit my holdings will likewise experience anticipation of the securement of their corresponding happiness. The relationship between property and happiness is therefore much more complicated than simply the pleasure that ownership generates at a specific moment, and its permanence is therefore vital.

In spite of his unambiguous endorsement of private property, Bentham retains his utilitarian scepticism of the absolute nature of all rights. Through his 'disappointment prevention principle', he is thus able to assert the necessity of ownership rights under normal circumstances, while at the same time maintain the need for the state to employ taxation to raise funds for the community under emergency conditions.[3] The role of this principle is to acknowledge that an absolute defence of private property will not always serve the public interest. Bentham's utilitarian justification of property therefore contains a robust flexibility in the face of changing empirical information to which his ideal legislator must respond.

We find a quite different utilitarian approach to the concept of property in J. S. Mill's *Principles of Political Economy* (1848), which he revised several times during his life and which would become the most influential textbook of nineteenth-century economics.[4] In this text, Mill expresses real worries about the capitalist economic system of his time, and reveals some apparent sympathy with the communistic rejection of private property ownership. As Mill considers the economic world that he inhabits, he bemoans a society that is full of 'sufferings and injustices' (1994a: 14), going so far as to suggest that many of the problems typically ascribed to communism are actually more likely to be found in an economic regime based on private ownership. Thus, for example, he considers and rejects the view held by Bentham that while communism encourages idleness, the contrary logic of capitalism provides incentives for individuals to 'reap the benefit of their own exertions' (10). Mill dismisses such a notion outright: within the capitalist society in which he finds himself, all workers – from immigrant labourer to government minister – expend their energies for wages and salaries that are fixed, which then means that they have no 'personal interest' or incentivising stake in the fruits of their exertions (10). He contrasts this with arrangements in an appropriately small-scale socialist society, where 'a workman labouring on his *own* account' would 'probably be more energetic than ... a labourer for hire' (11). If having a stake in the produce of one's labour functions as a suitable carrot, Mill suggests communism could also include a more effective stick than exists within capitalism. He speculates that, unlike under capitalism, in a socialist economy 'each labourer would be under the eye not of one master, but of the whole community', and thus would feel a more powerful sense of obligation to contribute productively (11). Mill concludes that the criticisms levelled at socialism are 'not necessarily insuperable' and judges the potential of humankind to be such as to make it obviously preferable to capitalism in 'the present state of society' (14).[5]

Despite his worries about the capitalism of his day, which he regarded as scarred by inequalities, poverty, and tragically squandered human potential, Mill nevertheless maintains that 'the principle of private property has never yet had a fair trial in any country' (1994a: 15). Furthermore, he thinks that there is a compelling case for it. The lack of a fair hearing for private ownership relates, he thinks, to its inauspicious origins. Property was not established from some initial situation of fairness or agreed social convention (as the natural law theorists wrongly imply), but rather through illegitimate means of 'conquest and violence' (15). Mill's view is that 'the laws of property have never conformed to the principles on which the justification of private property rests' (15). Such a conclusion will be of no surprise to readers of Rousseau. While the thievery that characterises its historical beginnings may undermine the *current* legitimacy of the institution, Mill's argument is that such origins do not threaten its rightness under *ideal* conditions. In other words, we should not rush to dismiss private property merely because of what we see around us, or because of the questionable roots of specific ownership rights.

In his theoretical defence of private property, he asks us to assume two necessary conditions for its rightness: the first is the 'universal education' of the community in question and the second is 'a due limitation of the numbers' of people therein. Since neither of these conditions obtain in nineteenth-century Britain, the case against private property – put forward by the socialist critics with whom Mill was familiar – fails as a matter of principle. Mill thinks that, under ideal circumstances, private ownership is perfectly justifiable and consequently he treats its legitimate existence as a 'fact' during his economic analysis in *Principles* (1994a: 46). Assuming the existence of his two specified conditions, he offers a utilitarian account of private ownership that departs from that advanced by Bentham. As one would expect from any utilitarian account, Mill asserts that 'property is only a means to an end, not itself the end' (33). For him, because the natural world was 'the original inheritance of the whole species', it follows that 'its appropriation is wholly a question of general expediency' (40–1) and does not relate to any moral right or obligation to acquire (or create) things through labour or otherwise. The utilitarian end in question – in line with Mill's broader ethical and political writings – is human freedom and moral development.[6] Provided there is a sufficiently educated community of a limited size, the existence of private ownership is conducive to human happiness and individual and social progress.

Mill's utilitarian theory of ownership encourages him to recommend limitations and conditions on the bundle of rights that the institution entails. These limitations mean that his conception of ownership strays from Bentham's insistence that a concern with equality must always yield to security. The role that equality has as an occasional check on ownership stems from Mill's very definition of property, which includes limitations on the sorts of things eligible for private acquisition. For Mill, the 'essential principle of property' is 'to assure to all persons what they have produced by their labour and accumulated by their abstinence'. Much follows from this terse definition and Mill's view of its broader political meaning. For one thing, this essential principle implies that the category of ownership cannot include 'what is *not* the produce of labour, the raw material of the earth' (1994a: 37, emphasis added). Like Locke and Paine before him, Mill's view here seems to be that individual labour is of sufficient moral significance to justify property rights. His reasons for holding this view are somewhat uncertain, since he does not offer a proper explanation of the connection between labour and ownership. He does not fully explain why the creation of something from the natural world inevitably belongs to its individual creator. This issue is especially important for him, since the community could potentially derive significant utility from *shared* ownership of whatever thing has been created.

Given the overall framework of his theory, an obviously reasonable inference would be that Mill regards labour as important because of the utility involved in the activity. Perhaps labour adds so much to the value of the natural world through its creative force that incentives to undertake it – and acquire individualised rights from it – become so valuable as to eclipse any utility found in a communistic alternative. Regardless of how he justifies the right of an owner to the produce of his labour, the distinction Mill draws between what counts as such (the property created) and what is instead the raw material of the earth has interesting entailments for the ownership of land. One of these is that when the relevant labourer/proprietor 'ceases to be the improver, political economy has nothing to say in defence of landed property' (1994a: 39). This seemingly radical claim implies the potential curtailment of both intra- and inter-generational transfers of owned portions of the natural world. The logical entailment would appear to be that whenever a person sells, exchanges, or bequeaths property to someone whose labour was not involved in its creation, the state could legitimately interfere, presumably in the name of utility. Mill's view is indeed that there is no necessary problem with the state confiscation of land should utility demand it, as long as it provides appropriate compensation. He also notes that a person's right over land does *not* include the right to *exclude* others from accessing it when they need to. Furthermore, Mill is explicit that if the land in question is not held for the purpose of cultivation, then 'no good reason can in general be given for its being private property at all' if the ownership fails to benefit the community (43). Such conditions show that Mill's account of utility shapes the nature of property rights, as well as justifying their existence.

The utilitarian account of property advanced by Mill – seemingly unfriendly towards the inviolability of landed property rights, but defensive of entitlements acquired through labour – also leads him to a quite distinct view of the transfer of owned holdings. Private ownership, for him, includes 'a right to the exclusive disposal' of holdings 'received either by gift or fair agreement' (Mill 1994a: 25).[7] As in the case of property acquired through labour, Mill thinks that holdings gained through consensual transfer are vulnerable to state interference on grounds of general utility. This vulnerability is particularly marked in the case of posthumous transfers. Unlike Bentham – who seems to follow Hume's incentive-based consequentialist reasoning on the topic – Mill rejects the idea of inheritance as an outdated expression of a feudal perspective that has no place in a political community in which the *individual* is the primary 'unit of society' rather than families or clans (1994a: 29). Mill does allow that children have a right to a share of the property of their parents for as long as they be in physical need, but that is as far as their entitlement extends. Though critical of inheritance, Mill nevertheless regards the power to bequeath one's holdings after death – and so to direct the destiny of those holdings to individuals of one's choosing – as a necessary part of the right to property. For him, without bequest 'the ownership of a thing cannot be looked upon as complete' (33). Even here, however, Mill observes utilitarian limitations. For example, while he believes that a testator should be permitted to specify that their bequest be used to establish a school, that same person's stated wishes about the lessons taught in that institution need not be honoured, should they conflict with the public good.

Though he identifies bequests as a necessary component of private ownership, Mill also thinks that they can be subject to appropriate taxation. In his explanation of the justness of taxation on posthumous transfers, he distinguishes between the power to bequeath and the right to *receive* a bequest. Mill thinks that protection of the right to give is legitimate, whereas the right to receive can be regulated using state taxation. This distinction is a practical one and does not really involve a meaningful moral or legal difference between the two statuses involved. A curtailment of the right of the recipient inevitably involves *some* restriction of the power to bequeath because it is the testator's intended transfer that is subjected to external interference. Mill's argument for taxation on the receipt of bequests relates back to his under-developed account of the role of labour in justifying specific ownership rights. His claim is that because the ownership of private property has a moral connection to labour, the convention of holdings being 'transmitted' to individuals 'without any merit or exertion of their own' should be judged 'not of the essence of the institution' and thus vulnerable to taxation for the greater good (Mill 1994a: 16). We must regard the receipt of such holdings by those who have not exerted their labour as 'a mere incidental consequence' of personal choice, and if such a decision has a negative impact on the well-being of the community as a whole then it can be restricted (16). Mill, like Hume, believes that the purpose of allowing posthumous transfers of property is ultimately to encourage virtuous behaviour, such as the hard work required to generate wealth.[8]

We can observe a glaring contradiction in Mill's attitude to bequest, which reveals much about his view of property in general. For him, as noted, ownership of something cannot be thought 'complete' unless it includes the power to bequeath and yet, at the same time, he insists that such an entitlement cannot be thought part of the 'essence' of property. Such oscillation ends with a characteristically utilitarian conclusion. The upshot, for Mill, is that 'the power of bequest may be exercised as to conflict with the permanent interests of the human race' (1994a: 34) and should therefore, where appropriate, be regulated by the state. Mill's solution to the problem of the potential unhappiness likely caused by the inegalitarian implications of large bequests is to use taxation to place limits on what can be received (35). He defends this proposal on various utilitarian grounds, which include a worry that excessive concentrations of wealth lead inevitably to undesirable inequalities of power. For him, both the very nature of property as a social institution and its necessary limitations are rooted quite explicitly in considerations of utility.

Evaluating the utilitarian theories of property

Despite the apparent antipathy of utilitarianism towards the concept of rights, we have seen how theorists within the utilitarian tradition have sought to develop robust defences of private property. The various arguments of Hume, Bentham, and Mill each justify individual property rights on the basis that their existence is conducive to the general good in some demonstrable way. For Hume, the existence of property is a fundamental element of peaceful social existence, emerging alongside morality, the force of which it helps cement. For Bentham, property is key to the security that is a necessary condition for all other forms of human happiness: its prominence within a commercial economy has been the culmination of our move away from primitive misery and is vital for banishing any temptation towards laziness. For Mill, private property is – under ideal conditions – assuredly in the interests of the human species, enabling our development, though its ownership should be managed through appropriately judged regulations for it to live up to its promise.

The utilitarian framework has clear intuitive resonance when it comes to justifying property, as it does for other social institutions. The everyday nature of private ownership encourages us to think of it as something that promotes more good outcomes than harmful ones and our initial conclusion is perhaps that it can be justified on such a basis. In accepting a utilitarian normative theory, we can defend property rights without recourse to any assumption about natural rights, the existence of which might look far more controversial (whether we prefer Locke or Nozick) than the easily accessible idea of happiness. For a proper evaluation, we need, however, to be attentive to the specificities of any utilitarian justification, and each of the theories we have surveyed in this chapter has distinct criticisms to answer. Even if we put aside any objections to Hume's sweeping historical-sociological description of the coincidental emergence of morality and property, we still might wish to resist the inescapably conservative structure of his justification of ownership. Hume's explanation of the utility of property mirrors that of other moral and political conventions that he discusses in his writing – such as the keeping of promises – in that it is retrospective in its structure. He looks at our political universe and seeks an explanation for the utility of what exists; and he concludes that we know it has utility, at least in part, because it exists and displays an apparent social function. The sustained nature of its existence invites a vindicatory account of its success, which Hume provides. One difficulty with this retrospective approach to evaluation is that – when taken in terms of utility – it stymies the possibility of critique and reform because of its potential resistance to any alternative (unverifiable) vision of the future.

The shakiness of Hume's account of inheritance provides a good illustration of this challenge. Worries about the inequalities of power that accompany unchecked intergenerational transfers do not seem to make sense within the Humean framework. The reason is that Hume explains the value of the institution of inheritance with ultimate reference to its usefulness. Yet when it comes to the verification of this usefulness – the question of how we are able to know that the allegedly virtuous conduct *is* causally traceable to the institution and is, in fact, useful – the very existence of the practice of inheritance is supposed to be sufficient. We know that institutions like property exist because of their utility, and if they were not friendly to utility then in all likelihood they would not have been sustained. Although there is an undeniable intuitive attraction to unpacking the things we associate with the practices and institutions that surround us, the reasoning here will look dangerously circular to those who are sceptical of the claims at issue. Hume's account of property can provide much in the way of comfort for its defenders, but perhaps no more comfort than is available for any other existing social institution. In the face of radical criticism of ownership from the anarchist or socialist – likewise often couched in consequentialist terms, as it invokes the suffering involved in the poverty generated by its existence – the defender of individual property rights might understandably desire a stronger set of arguments. The problem with Hume's argument is that while it seduces us with the authority that comes with empirical certainty, it seems to deny the possibility of refutation, which is supposed to be an implicit part of consequentialist reasoning.

The alternative utilitarian theories of Bentham and Mill do not face this challenge of circularity, but – as revealed by their substantive divergences – it is precisely the flexibility of their theories relative to that of Hume's which leaves them vulnerable to empirical challenges about the assured contribution of private ownership to human happiness. Bentham and Mill both agree that utility justifies property, but disagree about why and therefore also about the conditions that the state can place on legitimate ownership. The most obvious point of contention between them concerns the extent to which private property should be susceptible to redistributive measures to reduce material inequalities or alleviate poverty. Although both thinkers would no doubt insist that such questions of policy demand detailed attention to the utility at stake, we saw that they had rival beliefs about the normative values such attention should privilege. Bentham is strongly committed to the view that security must trump equality and that the role of property in vanquishing the constant threat of laziness justifies this. Bentham's view, like that of Hume, provides limited comfort to those in search of a compelling justification for private ownership. We must accept not only his claim that the conditions experienced in the pre-proprietary state are necessarily worse than those of the poor in advanced capitalism, but also, and crucially, that any ownership arrangements imagined – but as yet untested – that were *not* private would inevitably be deleterious of human happiness. His justification of property is thus vulnerable to changes in empirical circumstances. While many will regard this as an advantage, it is undeniable that his normative commitment to property is less robust as a result.

Mill's position is quite different again, since he believes the legitimate existence of property requires the meeting of quite strict conditions, including addressing the inegalitarian implications that are at stake. In his case, as the example of bequest shows, utilitarianism demands that a balance be struck – between permission and taxation – so that property can fulfil its function of encouraging the moral development of the individual and the creation of wealth for the community. Mill's argument looks hampered, not so much by the fact of its flexibility in the face of empirical concerns, but more immediately by the importance that he attaches to labour as an activity. Mill clearly thinks that labour is a morally significant activity, since it is what establishes the legitimacy of an individual property right and, in turn, explains why land itself (not being the creation of labour) should not be an object of exclusive ownership. It is much less clear, however, why Mill regards labour as important at all. Although the most likely explanation of its importance lies in the utility it generates, such an attitude looks hard to sustain without some kind of Lockean account of its value. His view is that property is justified by its expediency in promoting the greater good, but we might wish to doubt the connection between this end and the ascription of rights based on labour. Moreover, if labour is so crucial for the generation of utility, there seems no reason to think that an exclusive right to private property is an appropriate way to recognise this fact. Indeed, the permanence – absence of term – that customarily accompanies property ownership over a holding surely obtains *regardless* of labour, which would be odd if this is what secures private rights to it. Mill is himself aware of this disconnection, which is why he is suspicious of an unchecked power to bequeath. Would it not then be more conducive to Mill's utilitarian priorities to endorse ownership arrangements that are vulnerable to alterations in observed behaviour? If labour is so important, then should not Mill be committed to a patterned distribution of goods that tracks and rewards it? Such a conditional and temporary conception of ownership would be consistent with his attitude to bequest, where the state can legitimately interfere in the name of the greater good. Of course, were Mill's theory to admit openness to the possibility that the value of labour can be assured in some way other than permanent ownership, then it would no longer have any real purchase beyond that of a general utilitarianism, because rights become vulnerable to (potentially sudden) shifts in observable social reality.

Conclusion

Mill's theory illustrates that utilitarian approaches to property have an inherent flexibility that the libertarian tradition would appear to lack. This fact, in itself, lends it an attractiveness. We can acknowledge that the social world houses a number of moral practices and political institutions that together instantiate a plurality of normative commitments which, if considered discretely, might appear in tension with each other. As noted in the introduction, analysis of property as a concept seems inevitably to intrude upon conversations about the nature of liberty and equality. We cannot have a fruitful discussion of property in complete isolation from these concepts. Perhaps utilitarianism has the flexibility to accommodate these values and yield to either one, dependent on particular contextual circumstances and available empirical evidence. Despite its immediate attractiveness, however, we can also appreciate the weaknesses in any utilitarian justification of ownership. These weaknesses lie in its apparent inability to offer a sufficiently robust defence of private ownership – one that suggests the vital importance of the institution – in the face of the anarchist and socialist complaints we addressed in the first chapter.

Although some may conclude that the utilitarian justification of private property is the best we are going to get, its deficiencies also give us every reason to maintain the search for a superior one.

5

Ownership as Will in the World: Hegel's Account of Property

As I observed in the introduction, the nature of rights is such that they regulate interpersonal interaction. In doing so, they distribute *freedoms*: individual rights generate duties of non-interference for others, which permit the rights holder to exercise her liberty in certain ways. If I have a right to a patch of land conventionally identified as my garden, you have (under normal circumstances) a corresponding duty not to trespass on it by pitching a tent there, absent my consensual waiving of that duty. The rights we have over our holdings permit us to act in certain ways without interference. As discussed in the context of Nozick's theory, libertarianism gains much of its rhetorical appeal by explicitly linking its defence of property to a defence of the priority of individual freedom. Ownership rights provide us with the freedom to use, transfer, or simply possess holdings.

Freedom is, as noted earlier, a keenly contested concept within political philosophy. Scholars cannot even agree on its basic character, with some arguing that it is a starkly descriptive concept (such that being free is the physical predicate of an action) and others, by contrast, insisting that it is a more demanding political concept (and therefore being free refers to an existential condition with mental as well as physical elements). One of the most unusual and arresting accounts of freedom to be found in modern political thought is that put forward by the nineteenth-century German philosopher G. W. F. Hegel, in his most political work, *The Philosophy of Right* (1820). Therein, he connects freedom and property in a radically different way than does the libertarian tradition. Hegel's political philosophy is notoriously intricate and complex, and we inevitably do some violence to it by isolating specific parts of it for consideration without a comprehensive discussion and appreciation of its whole, for which we have insufficient space.[1] Nevertheless, in any critical appraisal of the most important theoretical justifications of ownership within Western political thought, it would be even more of a travesty to ignore Hegel's contribution to thinking about property rights – so we can proceed cautiously.

In his political theory, Hegel weaves together the tasks of justification and explanation, arguing that an adequate version of the latter is essentially equivalent to the former. He is concerned, in other words, to show *why* property exists as an institution and, by extension, has no apparent interest in considering arguments advanced *against* its existence. This disinterest stems from his belief that such viewpoints would imply a fundamental misunderstanding of the nature of social and political life. For Hegel, the job of philosophy is an essentially conservative one: its practitioners should *not* see their role as '*issuing instructions* on how the world ought to be' (1991: 23), but rather that of assembling a '*reconciliation with actuality*' (22), an account of the rationality, meaning, and value inherent in the society that surrounds us. An adequate philosophical understanding of the world is one that explains the rationality of it, as it exists, rather than one that interrogates established arrangements with a view to radical readjustment in line with abstract principles. That is not to say that Hegel's approach has much in common with the conservative utilitarianism of Hume. Hegel is not concerned to justify the existence of the social and political institutions that surround us through reference to their *usefulness*. There is no place in his theory for the idea that property is justifiable purely because it serves to satisfy the particular desires of individuals or improve the general welfare of society as a whole. Indeed, Hegel is explicit that were we to mistakenly ascribe needs as 'primary' in our explanation of the value of property, we will inevitably regard its possession 'as a means' to some kind of end, rather than as 'an essential end for itself' (77), which is how he thinks of it. He is, in general, suspicious of utilitarian arguments: as he observes – during his discussion of monarchy – 'the point of view of utility does not get us far ...', for it is always possible to point to disadvantages' of established social institutions (325). We earlier noted the susceptibility of utilitarian accounts of private ownership to the empirical experience or perception of such disadvantages. An account of needs, or usefulness, cannot explain the value of property, nor can it provide a means to justify particular instances of ownership or acquisition. Hegel's aim is instead to point out the important role that social and political institutions play in enabling the development of freedom and the historical unfurling of human consciousness.

Property as freedom

The uninitiated are likely to find Hegel's remarks on property to be at best enigmatic and at worst impenetrable. Some of his oblique declarations concerning the idea of ownership include the following statements: 'not until he has property does the person exist as reason' (1991: 73); 'from the point of view of freedom, property, as the first *existence* [*Dasein*] of freedom, is an essential end in itself' (77); and, perhaps most crucially, 'my will, as personal and hence as the will of an individual [*des Einzelnen*], becomes objective in property' (77). Each of these statements expresses a similar viewpoint about the *basicness* and *centrality* of property within the ethical development of the individual that Hegel charts in *The Philosophy of Right*. What they mean beyond that is, at first glance, less graspable. By the end of this chapter, the meaning of each statement – and the significance of terms such as 'objective' in the context of property – should be clearer and their appearance in this context less strange.

The story Hegel tells about freedom – of which property is but a minor part in a much larger whole – is a *developmental* one. It begins with analysis of human consciousness considered in its most abstract existence. It then traces the instantiation of consciousness in what he calls its 'ethical life' (the spheres of morality, the family, and civil society that characterise our social existence), which is then reconciled to its political home of the modern state, located within an account of world history driven towards a teleological end. The discussion of property takes place towards the beginning of the story of consciousness and before Hegel even gets to the ethical life of individuals – its basicness is such that it is part of his preceding account of '*abstract* right'. Within this abstract sphere, he outlines the idea of 'personality', which begins when the individual becomes aware not just of their particular intentionality – their own specific beliefs and desires – but also of their ability to control and change their character and behaviour. Personality is an awareness of our own subjectivity and the agency that we are capable of wielding; it is our realisation that causal laws do not purely govern us, unlike other parts of the natural world (Hegel 1991: 68). One becomes conscious of one's personality when one sees oneself as more than a mere animal, as a being that is able to exert control over one's person and the external world, rather than as a creature enslaved by biological needs or drives. Personality is, for Hegel, a uniquely human capacity. One of the definitive characteristics of personality is its initial *separateness* from the rest of the world: the realisation of our personality is a realisation of our uniqueness as an 'I' in the world, as distinct from others. For Hegel, this individual uniqueness and separateness from the rest of nature encapsulates the limitations of merely abstract personality and explains why we need to reach out to the external world to experience a meaningful existence. At this early stage of consciousness, we have not yet given any meaning to ourselves; our reality has no concreteness or substance when in the realm of abstract right. To overcome this mere abstract subjectivity, our personality – our will – must 'give itself reality', which means 'posit that existence [*Dasein*] as its own' in the world in such a way that it can be recognised as such by others (70). It is then this requirement to *express* our existence in reality that leads us towards freedom, most immediately through a world of individual rights where we establish our individuality as a socially recognisable fact.

The notion that freedom requires – and individual rights involve – an embrace of, as opposed to a protected retreat from, the external world, needs a bit of preliminary explanation. After all, such a view would run counter to the tradition of thinking of freedom as a physical *absence* of external interference. The first thing to note is that Hegel rejects the idea of *natural* rights – the conception of rights as entities that could somehow be meaningfully made sense of outside of a social context. For him, the idea of such natural rights implies, in political terms, a dangerous fanaticism, of the sort that followed the French Revolution (1991: 39). It is rooted in a misguidedly abstract, individualist view of reality and an impoverished understanding of freedom. For Hegel, a person whose consciousness floats (or aspires to float) freely above the social world, without the determinate commitments that accompany directed decisions – and their corresponding network of obligations – cannot be considered free in any real sense. We can only make sense of individual freedom, for Hegel, within the social matrices that give our lives meaning: to be properly free, we must project ourselves outwardly into the world through our will. We must deploy, express, and reveal our intentionality (the nature of our individual minds) through external action, rather than turn inwardly to our internal consciousness. What this implies, in less highfalutin terms, is a resistance to the commonplace notion that individuals are freer by having *more* choice or fewer tangible commitments. Although the idea of boundless choice is ostensibly seductive, as it appears to come with the promise of increased opportunity, Hegel's view is that it is, quite literally, vacuous. It is, for him, only through *making* choices (rather than *having* choices to make), and by directing and committing ourselves to projects and people, that we become free in any substantive sense. We must *embody* our freedom in the world through our social action.

Hegel's argument is that such embodiment requires that 'the person must give himself an external *sphere of freedom*' so that their subjectivity can be superseded, and their personhood therefore revealed to the world (1991: 73). It is at this point that property becomes necessary; as we will see, the very idea of freedom presupposes its existence. For Hegel, the phenomenon of property begins with the intentional act of outward projection, through which 'my inner act of will which says that something is mine must also become recognizable by others' (81). Through such externalisation the person in question will 'exist as reason', which is the state of establishing 'objective' status in the world. For freedom to be properly realised – to become *actualised* – and so not stay in a meaningless state of abstraction, the individual will must become determined; to exist fully, we must extend consciously into the external world making deliberate, observable choices. Through such choices, we reveal the aspects about ourselves that are unique. The imprint we make on the world through the conscious decisions we make – even down to what people might regard as mundane things like the clothes we choose to wear or whether we walk, drive, or take the bus – bestow our abstract forms with concrete particularity.

The extension of our will into the external world, crucially, secures our recognition by others, as a conscious person, with an identifiable and particular will. We reveal ourselves to others as a unique 'I' within this world. This external sphere we thrust ourselves into is the world of 'things', and the most basic way in which we can come to achieve our first experience of freedom here is through property. The establishment of property is not only a crucial step on the journey out of abstraction for individual self-consciousness, it also provides a concreteness to the external world, which will become transformed in individual minds from an arena of nature to one that bears the mark of human rationality and purpose. Hegel maps this journey across the whole of *The Philosophy of Right*, within which property serves as just the initial step out of abstraction. To recall, then, one of the enigmatic expressions highlighted earlier, we can already appreciate why property will emerge as the 'first *existence*' of the individual freedom that will then be more fully developed through its location in more complex social and political institutions.

Moments of ownership

At this stage, we need some illustration to bring us down from such lofty abstraction, to get a grip on both why Hegel regards property as so important and how a person first acquires ownership rights. He helpfully provides some examples to show the practical reality of how property functions to secure the externalisation of the will in the world and its necessary recognition by others. For Hegel, 'a person has the right to place his will in any thing' (1991: 75). He understands a thing to be any entity that lacks the self-consciousness that defines the human species.[2] When it comes to the issue of how particular things become legitimately owned by particular people, Hegel's theory does not ascribe any authority to the Lockean notion of initial acquisition based on the investment of labour. He does, however, take us through three key 'moments' of ownership: (1) taking possession, (2) use, and (3) alienation. These moments show how individual intentionality is manifest in property.

The *taking possession* of things requires (perhaps obviously) that they be unowned in the first place, as they would otherwise already constitute property and thus be unavailable for appropriation. Taking possession can involve the physical seizure of a thing or the mere designation of one's claim to it. We can choose, for instance, to cultivate an unowned plot of land, or we can register our possession by merely declaring it *mine* through putting up a sign that indicates it (Hegel 1991: 84). Both such actions enable us to display our will – our individual intentionality – to others in the world, such that it can be recognised: our status as an 'I' is connected to our action in the material world. The mere physical appropriation of a thing is, as Hegel acknowledges, an unsophisticated way of revealing one's will through property; after all, the simple acquisition of something does not necessarily reveal very much about our intentionality. Taking possession is a purposeful action, but the purpose underlying it can be unsatisfyingly basic. We can thus also use our will, with far more effect, to *give form* to a thing through our possession, choosing to mould an object in a way that reflects our intentionality. By giving form to a thing – even if this just means training our dog to follow instructions, or physically manipulating ice to create a sculpture – we are putting our will into the world in a manner that is both deliberate and observable by others (1991: 86).

The second exemplary moment of property as will-in-the-world is the *use* of a thing. As noted, Hegel attaches no importance to the satisfaction of needs in his justification of property: the usefulness of property does *not* explain the value of ownership. The significance of use does not lie in the fact that it serves an individual need – such as sustenance, which is a mere animal requirement – but rather that an individual has identified, acted on, and therefore expressed a particular desire *through* that use. It is thus not the need satisfied, but the desire revealed and then advertised to others that makes use important. When I use a thing to satisfy my desires, as when I form a thing, I am subduing it to my will. Nature again bears the imprint of our individual intentionality and this physical manifestation of our will is recognisable by other wills. Hegel describes the phenomenon of use almost as though it were a battle between a person's will and nature, with the human mind successfully exerting its power and rendering visible its dominance of the world. Through use, the thing is 'negated' by the person in this moment of dominance:

> the thing is reduced to a means of satisfying my need. When I and the thing come together, one of the two must lose its [distinct] quality in order that we become identical. But I am alive, a willing and truly affirmative agent; the thing, on the other hand, is a natural entity. It must accordingly perish, and I survive ... (Hegel 1991: 89)

The exemplar of such a perishing is, on Hegel's view, when a person slaughters and consumes a non-human animal. In so doing, a person both displays their will in the world and overcomes a thing through vanquishing it – indeed, it is by vanquishing it, and thus revealing its nature *as* a thing, that the individual's will is revealed to the social world.

The third exemplary moment of ownership in the world observed by Hegel is the *alienation* of property – that is, we assure our property with our decision to *abandon* what we own through a variety of means. 'True alienation' is, for Hegel, 'a declaration by the will that I no longer wish to regard the thing as mine' (1991: 95). For him, the alienation of a thing reveals the fact of our ownership to the world in an important way. This sounds like a paradoxical suggestion. How can it be true that the alienation of a thing – the fact that we purposefully relinquish our ownership of it – provides an exemplification of our property? For Hegel, the answer is that alienation does not simply involve the *removal* of our will from the thing that we have come to own. It rather exemplifies our will in action: by *choosing* purposefully to alienate a piece of property, a person is necessarily exerting control over it. That person is directing the destiny of an object – we are again displaying our will in a publicly recognisable way. Alienation is thus a key part of property as a vehicle for externalising our will.

It is important to remember that when describing these moments of ownership, we are still in the realm of abstract right and these exemplifications of property as will in the world serve only to sketch the primal elements of ownership. They offer glimpses as to the character of property as a fully-fledged social institution, and capture the ways in which we express our personality through it and secure recognition by others. In the economic marketplace – a key part of Hegel's account of civil society within his broader vision of ethical life – there is no expectation on his part for individuals to be physically involved in acts of taking possession or giving forms to things. That said, we can certainly find analogous instantiations in modernity, and using the internet to acquire a bag of potatoes is, according to Hegel's reasoning, as much an expression of my will as growing them in a field. Furthermore, we do still find these seemingly primitive aspects of property even within much more complex social arrangements, as we can see in the case of posthumous transfers. During his discussion of the raising of children and the dissolution of the family, Hegel makes clear his opposition to any notion of a power to bequeath held by a property owner (the 'right to make a will'), in favour of a contrary right to inheritance held by dependents, which he endorses as crucial for social cohesion (1991: 215).

Hegel dismisses any discretionary right to bequest because it, by definition, leaves the choice to dispose of one's property in the hands of an individual testator. Such choices can be entirely capricious, arbitrary, and random and they therefore lack any necessary ethical credibility. One's mere preferences are, for Hegel, unreliable, and an attachment of importance to them harks back to the perverted belief that an increased arena for our choice (as opposed to an increase in our choices *made*) gives us more freedom. Although this attitude might seem in conflict with his previous emphasis on the significance of the alienation of one's property as an excellent outlet for the expression of will, he actually defines inheritance as 'essentially a *taking possession* by the individual as his own property of which in themselves are [within the family] common resources' (1991: 214, emphasis added). The complexity of inheritance – with whatever detailed rules and regulations might accompany it as a legal practice – is ascribed significance, in part, because of its atavistic encapsulation of taking possession of property within a specific context – within a family unit, following the death of its head.

It has been suggested by some commentators (e.g. Garnsey 2007: 149) that Hegel's account of property is 'to some extent indebted to Locke' as far as the 'concept of self-ownership' is concerned. The grounds for drawing comparisons between the two appear in Hegel's account of alienation. As with Locke, Hegel thinks that I 'can *alienate individual* products of *my particular physical and mental [geistigen] skills* and active capabilities to someone else' through selling my labour '*for a limited period*' (1991: 97). The period of labour must be limited – and must be, in principle, revocable – because otherwise, I would be 'making the substantial quality of ... my personality itself, into someone else's property' and would be willing my own enslavement (97). When explaining the illegitimacy of voluntary slavery, Hegel's language does become somewhat Lockean, as when he writes that 'those goods ... which constitute my own distinct personality and the universal essence of my self-consciousness are ... *inalienable*, and my right to them is *imprescriptible*' (95).[3] These sentiments do sound reminiscent of the idea of self-ownership that we see in Nozickean libertarianism, which, as shown, has an ancestral (though very different) voice in

Locke's political theory. It would be, however, potentially misleading to make too much of this apparent similarity.

Uniting Locke and Hegel around the idea of self-ownership ignores what is distinct about their accounts of property ownership. For Hegel, property is necessary for the extension of one's personality into the world. It is through property that we reveal ourselves as agents with demonstrable intentionality. For Locke, acquisition is necessary to fulfil a duty of self-preservation. To flatten this distinction between their arguments – and to do so with reference to the atomistic idea of self-ownership, which both Locke and Hegel would surely baulk at, albeit for different reasons – seems wrong. Being clear about the distinction between the arguments of Locke and Hegel raises another issue about the *limitations* on ownership. Beyond the arena of abstract right and moving into the world of civil society and the state, Hegel's view is that there can be legitimate intrusion upon the right to property. Should the community require us to surrender our property in deference to a matter of more pressing importance, we must, Hegel thinks, be prepared to do so. He does maintain that the community cannot undertake any usurpation of the right to private property because of 'contingency, private arbitrariness, or private utility', but only in the name of 'the rational organism of the state' (1991: 77). Such assurances are nonetheless unlikely to give much comfort to individuals seeking security for their holdings, since it is not clear how frequently they might expect to endure such surrenders of ownership.

The broader question raised by such an ascription of power to a community over the individuals within it is whether Hegel is offering a theory of *private* property at all. It might not seem far-fetched to envisage the identified moments of ownership – and the externalisation and recognition they imply – experienced under some kind of communistic scheme. Even under schemes of joint ownership we can make sense of ideas of possession, use, and even (recalling the examples of altruism in Morris's utopian vision) giving things away to reflect our will. We have seen that Hegel is happy to countenance state interference with property rights under certain circumstances, and we know – via his rejection of bequests – that he can be quite suspicious of the trumping force of individual choice in certain situations. Does his account of property therefore necessarily imply its *exclusive* ownership by individuals with rights held against each other? The only way to answer this question is with reference to the importance of Hegel's concept of recognition. At first glance, the idea of recognition might not itself appear capable of generating a private property regime, but full consideration of its importance in Hegel's overall scheme explains how it does so. Although we have thus far been discussing externalisation of will as an individualised process – whereupon we achieve recognition of our own consciousness – it is actually the concept of *mutual* recognition that does the vital work in Hegel's theory. Such mutual recognition depends on the securement of private individual rights. The idea is not just that *I* am recognised as an individual, self-conscious, and responsible being, but that I come to recognise *others* as such as well. To be a person in the full sense of the concept requires the recognition of other persons. What we establish is a vast network of recognition, each seeing others as distinct agents in the world. It is through acknowledgement of the rights of others that we secure our own individual statuses as rights-bearing individuals. Our freedom is thus realised interdependently.

Property is the first, most basic step in the establishment of the network of rights: it is a necessary condition for the cementation of our moral and political status. All of our rights will come to depend on private ownership, as this basic step begins the process of mutual recognition. Such ownership *must* be private because of its connection to the contracts that individuals then make with each other. It is from his account of property that Hegel derives the idea of contract – where rights are transferred from one to another – which entails that a thing 'has *now* ceased to be my property, and that I already recognize it as the property of the other party', such that rights are established (1991: 109). To make sense of the alienation of my car to you, I must, for the transaction to make any sense, recognise you as an active will. This recognition is implicit in the very idea of a *private* contract, which, of course, requires both the exclusion of other agents and their simultaneous recognition of its validity. Contract then implies other links in Hegel's conceptual derivation: it (or rather its breach) generates an idea of wrong, the recognition of which then entails a notion of morality and the ethical life that characterises our social and political existences. Every link in the chain in the journey from abstract consciousness to concrete political institutions is necessary. We need all the surroundings of our social and political lives to secure our rights and therefore our freedom. Property is therefore of critical importance for Hegel's story. The very notion of mutual recognition (wherein our rights and freedom are established) is dependent upon it. This is not to say that Hegel's justification of property is somehow parasitic on contract, because that is the next link in the chain – it is not the need for contract that justifies property or vice versa. The point is rather that a proper appreciation of Hegel's explanation of private ownership requires attention to his philosophical system as a whole and the moral (and ontological) commitments that drive it. It is only by attending to his whole system that we can see the connection between property and freedom, and it is the idea of mutual recognition – the notion that we can successfully establish our own individuality in concert with others through social life – that most vividly connects the discrete stages in his account of politics.

Property and poverty: the problem of 'the rabble'

I have so far sketched Hegel's view that the institution of private property is vital for the individual. The ownership of property is important for the externalisation of will into the natural world, because it secures mutual recognition, meaningful freedom, and a system of individual rights anchored within a social context. This account is clearly distinct from any claim about a natural right to property (which, for Hegel, would make no sense because of an absence of appropriate social context) and from any utilitarian interest in the happiness or welfare of the individuals in question (which is irrelevant to his account). Given that property is of such huge significance in his political philosophy, we might assume that Hegel thinks that it is something that *every* individual should have. The claims that he makes about the importance of property are unequivocal and universal in character and he does not assign any weight to a particular mode of acquisition, such as labour. If property is the fundamental route for us to first reveal and express our individual wills – and if it provides the required impetus towards the larger network of rights that define his vision of right – there would seem to be a strong case for an economic system that secures property for *all*. Property, Hegel tells us, is both necessary and basic for human freedom, relevantly separating us from, and giving us means to command, the material world of mere things. Should a Hegelian polity not therefore ensure that there is property for all? Central to his understanding of civil society is the economic marketplace, which is a sphere of individual freedom ultimately protected and overseen by a powerful state. Should there be some substantial redistribution of property by that state to guarantee that the experience of the embodied freedom he celebrates spreads across society, rather than be restricted to only some of its members?

Despite his thesis about the intimate connection between the ownership of property and the development of human freedom, Hegel is actually opposed to any idea of a forced redistribution of holdings, especially if the purpose would be to serve some kind of egalitarian end (such as to promote the dignity of all through ownership rights). He is fundamentally suspicious of equality as a political ideal. We might, Hegel concedes, regard individuals as equal in terms of their 'abstract personality', but such an ascription is an 'empty and tautological' notion (1991: 80). Stripped of their particularity, human beings might be abstractly equivalent, but this sameness is of no moral significance. He rejects the idea that there could ever be *'equality* in the distribution of land or even of other available resources' as 'vacuous and superficial' (80). The basis for his rejection is that nature – being composed of things with no personality – cannot be a subject of just, or indeed any, distributive concern. For Hegel, the nature of property ownership is, by definition, resistant to any kind of distributive taming or patterning. The reason for this resistance is that the legitimate ownership of particular things is dependent on a huge number of variable factors, such as 'subjective ends, needs, arbitrariness, talents, external circumstances, etc.' (79). We come to own property in all kinds of ways that do not adhere to any one definition of deservingness or any singular kind of action. A community cannot police the rightness of who owns what by using abstract and external judgements about fittingness. Such judgements would make no sense – the notion of a centralised distribution of property is, on this account, a kind of category error, akin to trying to engineer a correct number of children within families by swapping them around at birth.

Any redistribution intended to establish or restore a distributive pattern would be contrary to the necessarily inegalitarian character of property as an institution. Hegel is at one with Nozick here. That said, during his rejection of equality as a meaningful political value, Hegel does appear to express the view that some redistribution of holdings may be morally required. He writes that 'it is false to maintain that justice requires everyone's property to be equal; for it [equality] requires only that *everyone should have property*' (1991: 81, emphasis added). He then repeats the same sentiments, adding that property holdings cannot be equal for the reasons already adduced, and that 'justice ... requires only that everyone should have property' (81). These pronouncements are potentially radical. Their implications would seem to hark back to the medieval and early-modern Christian natural law theories discussed earlier, which specified that everyone must have sufficient access to property to secure their survival. In fact, taken together with his description of the role of property in the development of human freedom, Hegel's declaration about the universality of property required by justice looks potentially even more demandingly egalitarian in distributive terms.

Does Hegel mean to suggest that the moral equality of each personality demands guaranteed property for every person? There is some ambiguity in *The Philosophy of Right* on this question, but the prospects for any redistributive reading are ultimately bleak. Although Hegel's view that 'everyone ought to have property' (1991: 81) is starkly expressed, he never explicitly endorses the idea of redistribution. Furthermore, there is abundant evidence available to indicate that he is *against* such redistribution. We have already addressed his case against state interference in private property in the name of equality. Perhaps even more telling is his attitude to poverty in civil society and his reluctance to offer any solution to it. Within his consideration of the nature of, and challenges to, civil society, Hegel identifies poverty as a real problem in modernity. Civil society is, for him, a vital and complex 'system of needs': it is an economic system that thrives on a delicate equilibrium of harnessed marketplace self-interest and personal investment in endeavours that promote solidarity within the community. Although Hegel is committed to the real value of the market in enabling human freedom, he is nevertheless aware of the dreadful poverty that can emerge from this organisation of economic life (265). His view is that it is imperative for the civic health of political societies that they establish ways and means of preventing or ameliorating such poverty.

Hegel is aware that just as the ownership of particular holdings is attributable to various actions and circumstances, so the emergence of poverty can have a number of different sources. These sources include the contingencies of the economic market, such as the vagaries of supply and demand, as well as sudden shifts in technology that alter the nature of production and work. For Hegel, an especially dangerous species of poverty can threaten the harmony of civil society. This poverty occurs when 'a large mass of people sinks below the level of a certain standard of living' and becomes what he calls 'a *rabble*' (1991: 266). The resultant poverty thrown up by the contingencies he identifies creates the conditions necessary for the rabble to emerge from the affected members of society. Hegel's worry about the development of the rabble is not about poverty *per se*. Indeed, the disposition or mentality that the rabble holds and displays is what defines the group, rather than any specific level of material indigence that the individuals within it experience. According to Hegel,

> Poverty in itself does not reduce people to a rabble; a rabble is created only by the disposition associated with poverty, by inward rebellion against the rich, against society, the government, etc. It also follows that those who are dependent on contingency become frivolous and lazy, like the *lazzaroni* of Naples, for example. This in turn gives rise to the evil

that the rabble do not have sufficient honour to gain their livelihood through their own work, yet claim that they have a right to receive their livelihood. (1991: 266)

For Hegel, the problem of the rabble arises not principally because of their material conditions, but rather because of the spirit of disenchantment that comes along with poverty. It is this debased demeanour – the 'disposition of laziness, viciousness, and other vices' (265) – that exercises him because it threatens to undermine the cohesion of civil society.

One of the curious aspects of Hegel's discussion of the rabble is his complete failure to resolve the problem he is so careful to identify.[4] For seemingly every dynamic movement in his derivation of conceptual categories, any problem noted is creatively resolved through a dialectic structure, because the problem itself is part of the overall philosophical project. For example, the problem of wrongful action generates its own solution by implying the need for a shared morality. He raises the problem of selfishness in the economic sphere of civil society only to resolve it through the presence of corporations and the corresponding spirt of solidarity within a community. Hegel even finds a rationality for the problem of war, as a necessary means of galvanising a state through patriotism on rare occasions. Poverty stands seemingly alone within his political philosophy as an urgent problem that he knows to be the creation of a staple element of his institutional vision – the economic marketplace – and yet does not offer any convincing account of how a society might deal with it. He is adamant (1) that this rabble that 'agitates and torments modern societies' (1991: 237) is the consequence of a *lack* of property, and (2) that everyone ought to own property for reasons covered above. An obvious potential solution to (1) might be to take (2) seriously through some kind of state redistribution. We know that Hegel thinks that such redistribution is contrary to the very nature of property, but we also know that it is, in fact, possible through a system of taxation – though it may not be viable or sensible to redistribute physical objects, having a currency as medium of exchange eases redistributive manoeuvres. The sceptical Hegelian retort would be that any such state redistribution through taxation would fail to respect the 'honour' of the beneficiary of the transfer because that individual would be treated as though a passive recipient of things rather than an active agent taking control of the world. It nevertheless would surely be the case that securing property rights for individuals who have none might provide them with at least the means to develop that honour and agency subsequently. It would also satisfy Hegel's claim that property be universal. But he does not entertain such a notion.

An alternative solution could be the mere augmentation of the rules governing property rights, along the lines found in the Christian conceptions of charity mentioned earlier. As we saw, even Locke's robust theory of property ownership contains a clause that seemingly licenses acts of what would otherwise be theft, through rights of acquisition triggered in circumstances of need so desperate that the preservation of human life is at stake. While this provision of charity might provide a way for Locke to defend property without allowing the poor to perish, Hegel rejects it outright as any solution to the problem of the rabble. Indeed, for him, giving alms to the rabble would simply make the situation of poverty even worse for civil society, for what will be familiar reasons. According to Hegel,

> if the direct burden [of support] were to fall on the wealthier class, or if direct means were available in other public institutions ... to maintain the increasingly impoverished mass at its normal standard of living, the livelihood of the needy would be ensured *without the mediation of work*; this would be contrary to the principle of civil society and the feeling of self-sufficiency and honour among its individual members. (1991: 267, emphasis added)

Hegel is here explicit: charity – whether it be from private individuals or the state – cannot be acceptable as a solution because it would feed the resentment of the rabble, rather than enabling them to overcome their condition through their own work and corresponding responsibility for their lives. The best way to deal with this situation is instead – as he thinks we can see from the terrible example of English Poor Laws and what he describes as 'limitless private charity' – 'to leave the poor to their fate and direct them to beg from the public' (1991: 267).

It would seem then, that on the one hand Hegel believes that everyone should own property and yet, on the other, he is just as insistent that those left without it cannot look to the state for direct assistance in getting any, even under economic conditions where their lack of ownership is attributable to the contingencies of the market. What are we to make of this significant tension in his political theory? Perhaps Hegel's failure to square the universal importance of property ownership with the existence of a class of people without access to it is to be expected. Maybe we can explain it with reference to the other aspects of his political thought that appear contradictory when viewed from the perspective of twenty-first-century liberalism. The key philosophical commitment that defines contemporary liberalism – and which unites theorists as politically distant from each other as Nozick and Cohen – is arguably to a conception of basic human moral equality: the idea that any legitimate normative theory must, in some respect, acknowledge the equal moral status of those individuals who will be subject to political authority.

This fundamental commitment seems occasionally visible in Hegel's writing – after all, his philosophical analysis of politics is explicated with reference to *personality* and *will* and other abstract, individual, and universal categories that would seem to imply the existence of a human unit with some kind of notional equal status. Attention to such terms is what makes us think that there is something telling in his assertion that *everyone* should have property. It would be wrong, however, to think that Hegel is committed to the same egalitarian premises that ground twenty-first-century liberal theories, and not only because of his aforementioned dismissal of equality as empty and tautological. He also expresses a number of notoriously inegalitarian and illiberal views. The last few pages of *The Philosophy of Right* provide a brief defence of colonialism: Hegel suggests that 'civilised nations' have the right 'to regard and treat as barbarians other nations which are less advanced than they are' (1991: 376). He regards women as fundamentally inferior to men: when compared to men, who resemble non-human animals in some situations, women are more akin to plants, whom, he speculates, appear to receive ideas in a state of placid submission rather than through intentional acquisition (207). His discussion of the patriarchal family unit is also a world away from the individualism we now associate with the modern liberal tradition.

The purpose of highlighting these inegalitarian and illiberal tenets contained in Hegel's writing is not to anachronistically bludgeon his intellectual legacy with moral and political assumptions that he would not recognise. It is rather to suggest that we should not necessarily view his theory of property as contradictory when we approach it with twenty-first-century eyes. Once we abandon our modern liberal presuppositions, we can consider the possibility that while Hegel asserts that *everyone* should hold property, his vision of those people who comprise the moral and political universe departs radically from ours. At the same time, this observation does not render his account of merely antiquarian interest. One apparent virtue of Hegel's theory is that it embeds a defence of the value of property firmly within a broader set of normative commitments, such that it does not require – as with the case of self-ownership – independent justification in the face of a striking clash with other cherished moral ideas. It seems reasonable to ask what Hegel's theory of property would look like were it to incorporate the liberal presuppositions that characterise contemporary political philosophy. We might see a plausible account of a right to private property within an overall system that has the capacity to solve the problem of poverty that it acknowledges exists in a world of exclusive ownership.

Conclusion

It might seem that – as with the utilitarian account of the concept – Hegel's argument for property stands or falls in accordance with the strengths or weaknesses of a broader theoretical framework that we can evaluate only holistically. Property is, for him, a fundamentally important institution because it provides the first step towards the externalisation of individual will and its corresponding embodiment and mutual recognition in the material world that it shapes and masters. In contrast to Rousseau's damning critique of commercial society, Hegel thinks that our exclusive ownership of things – manifest in various ways – is morally valuable because of how it allows us to reveal and develop our personality at various stages of our conscious existence. It begins from our initial taming of nature and continues with the specific individual choices and commitments that we make within civil society.

It should be clearer why Hegel regards the individualistic freedom associated with the natural rights tradition as being completely 'arbitrary' in terms of what it licenses and endorses. For him, the notion that freedom means simply doing what we please, or of having as few constraints as possible, is revelatory of nothing more than 'a complete lack of intellectual culture' (Hegel 1991: 48). The alternative conception of freedom he articulates is one that instead has a concrete relationship to (rather than a protected distance from) the external world. His conception of freedom does not imply that Ronaldo is made freer when untaxed by political authority and nor does it imply that an egalitarian redistribution of property will generate more overall freedom within a society. For Hegel, property does not *increase* freedom, or the opportunities to act freely; it rather *embodies* freedom by enabling the externalisation of an individual will into the world in such a way that other agents can recognise it. The question for modern readers is whether, if that vision of freedom is an attractive one, and if everyone ought to have property, it must imply some commitment to economic redistribution to retain its coherence and plausibility.

6
Property within Justice: Rawls and Beyond

In the preceding chapters, we have considered various justifications for private property as a social institution. The arguments that have underpinned these justifications have each had some intuitive purchase and their premises have often been, at first glance, quite attractive. Each of the theories examined so far also face significant challenges to their plausibility and coherence. Nozick's libertarianism seems to defend property at all costs, regardless of how it undermines our moral outrage at the situation of the desperately needy – property is (via self-ownership) apparently *all* that matters in his normative universe, at the expense of interest in both equality and freedom, a commitment that renders it an ultimately unsatisfying worldview. Utilitarian theories appear to have the precisely opposite problem, insofar as they justify the existence of property with reference to a separate end to be achieved, such that their consequent subservience to other values surrenders the specificity of property as a political concept. Property here ends up with a necessarily insecure foundation because it is nothing more than a slave to utility. Of the approaches we have canvassed, Hegel's theory perhaps comes closest to an account of property that successfully explains its distinct conceptual value and simultaneously embeds it within an overall normative system. Yet his theory is not without problems, as it cannot reconcile the universal importance of property with his inability to respond to the problem of poverty, which, as he acknowledges, is a consequence of the market economy.

In recent years, political philosophers have sought increasingly to defend the idea of property within a holistic theory that integrates our various normative commitments, such that it is not competing with (or justified by) rival conceptions of liberty, equality, utility, or any other value we might cherish. Advocates of this holistic approach believe that property can only be justified within an overall theory of *justice*. In outlining their conceptions of ownership, these theorists have sought explicitly to address the tensions – identified in our first chapter in the critiques put forward by anarchist and socialist writers – between property and poverty, and to show how an amelioration of the latter is addressable through a specific understanding of the former. In this final chapter, I turn to the attempt to theorise property as *part of* an account of economic justice.

Rawls on the right to private property

Although the integration of the concept of property within broader normative theories of justice is prominent within contemporary political philosophy, it is not in itself novel. In the first chapter, we encountered Rousseau's devastating critique of the degraded nature of commercial modernity, which is characterised, for him, by an intolerable inequality enabled by the institution of private property. Given Rousseau's valorisation of human existence before modernity – where 'natural man' lived freely and without corruption – it seems reasonable to expect him to recommend a wholesale renunciation of ownership as an institution, a complete abolition of the legal categories of yours and mine. Despite his attack on the legitimacy of property rights and his apparent view that the establishment of private ownership as an institution would depend on 'the express and unanimous consent of Humankind', Rousseau does *not* advocate a reversion to the communism that allegedly characterised our primitive, pre-social state. He regards such a reversion as impossible. In fact, in *The Social Contract*, he actually offers an explicit *justification* of private property ownership. The conclusion he reaches in that text is that individual property rights are defensible (and legitimately protectable by the state) when they are held in a political community that is characterised by a broader commitment to justice and equality of citizens (Rousseau 1997b). According to Rousseau, private property rights can be a legitimate feature of a just society.

Rousseau's conclusion in *The Social Contract* is that those committed to civic equality can ultimately make their peace with the idea of ownership rights, through the social contract that is capable of binding a community together. For him, any justification of property becomes ultimately parasitic on a broader normative account of justice, such that it makes little sense to consider one without the other: we can situate exclusive rights to holdings within a society where there is political equality. Rousseau broad approach to political philosophy – his ambition to take 'men as they are and laws as they might be' – was an important influence on John Rawls's vision of a theory of justice. Rawls describes his Rousseauian account of the scope of such a theory as a *realistic utopia* (2001: 4). This label is supposed to capture the ambition to offer the most attractive normative theory available given the constraints on what might actually be possible in the world. Among the important components of Rawls's comprehensive and hugely ambitious political theory is his account of 'property-owning democracy'. Through this idea, he attempts to show how private property rights can protect both individual freedom and equality.

Although he wrote his earliest work on moral and political philosophy in the 1950s, Rawls's intellectual contribution to liberal thought continues to shape many scholarly conversations well into the twenty-first century, and none more so than debates about the nature of economic justice.[1] His first major work (*A Theory of Justice* (1999), published originally in 1971) outlines a normative theory that he spent the rest of his career further developing and refining. Central to his theory is – as the title of his book suggests – the idea of justice, which he describes as 'the first virtue of social institutions'. For Rawls, among all our various normative commitments, justice is the ultimate value; it is a basic standard of moral rightness that rules and institutions must meet in order to be legitimate. The essence of Rawls's theory – which he calls 'justice as fairness' – lies in the two principles he endorses. The first principle is concerned with what we can describe as the *social/political* aspect of justice and asserts the right to 'equal basic liberties' for all (Rawls 2001: 42). The purpose of this principle is to enable each individual to develop and pursue their own plan of life without constraint or censure from others. It maintains that no person can be compelled or coerced into certain actions or ways of living. The first principle protects, for example, our freedom of employment as well as our right to political participation, free expression, and so forth (45). The second principle relates more specifically to *economic* justice and the distribution of resources within a society. It has two distinct parts. The first part maintains that inequalities in a society are justified only insofar as they exist against a backdrop of 'fair equality of opportunity'. The second part – the 'difference principle' – stipulates that such inequalities are only acceptable if they are of benefit to the least-advantaged members of society (42–3). Economic inequalities are thus perfectly permissible, but only if (a) they are part of a system that is properly *fair* in terms of the access that individuals have to the advantages that they seek, and (b) that this system is organised so that the worst-off group are economically better off than they would be under any alternative arrangement.

Despite the vast scholarship devoted to Rawls's work, there has been – until recently – scant scholarly attention paid to his understanding of property. This might seem, at first, a bit peculiar, since his theory evidently offers an account of economic justice, one that is considerable in parallel with those put forward by Locke, Hume, and so on. The lack of interest in this aspect of Rawls's thought likely stems from his occasional treatment of the right to private property as something *separate* from his account of economic justice. Within the framework of justice as fairness, Rawls specifies and locates the right to property in relation to the *first* (social/political) principle of justice, rather than the more explicitly economically focused second. He presents 'the right to hold and to have exclusive use of personal property'

(2001: 114) as one of the equal basic rights and liberties to be guaranteed within a society, alongside the right to vote and freedom of association. It is reasonable to infer – from this asserted commitment to private property as a basic and fundamental right – that Rawls's first principle sets definite limitations to any subsequent account of economic justice. It seems that whatever the second principle will demand in terms of supporting equality, it needs first to respect exclusive rights of private ownership, against which any redistributive policies must be tempered. Such a conclusion gains credibility when we acknowledge that Rawls ascribes priority to the first principle over the second. This priority means that no sacrifice of any person's equal basic liberties can be countenanced *even if* doing so would support economic justice. For Rawls, we cannot justly deny basic liberties to the least-advantaged even if doing so would improve their economic position within it: it would not be acceptable, for example, to remove freedom of employment even if doing so increased resources for the poorest people. According such priority to the first principle makes it seem that Rawls is committed to private property as something protected from redistribution. It is, after all, a basic right.

For Rawls, the right to personal property is (at least in part) justified by the need 'to allow a sufficient material basis for personal independence and a sense of self-respect, both of which are essential for the adequate development and exercise of the moral powers' (2001: 114). The right to private property is evidently part of what it means to recognise an individual as a moral agent as well as an equal citizen: having exclusive entitlements over specific holdings helps individuals achieve some independence and ensures for them an appropriate status within their society, along with their fellows. In this respect, his view bears some resemblance to the Hegelian view of property as a necessary part of one's personality in the world, as a securement of one's freedom and individual standing in relation to others. Although Rawls expresses his commitment to individual property rights through his first principle of justice, his conception of ownership is not a typical one. After he identifies the right to own property – which he insists that 'all citizens have in virtue of their fundamental interests' – he then immediately qualifies it quite dramatically. He explains that the right does *not* extend to 'natural resources', nor does it imply the right to own or to participate equally in 'the control of the means of production', which includes 'rights of acquisition and bequest' (114). These characteristics of property, for him, do not count as 'basic' to the concept.

This basic conception of property appears radically different to the everyday understanding in Western liberal democracies and to the theories of ownership we have considered already.[2] Rawls's account specifies limitations on *what we can own*, by excluding natural resources (which might mean water or land), as well as undermining certain *forms of economic organisation* by excluding ownership rights over the means of production. Such a conception would seem at first to be unwelcome both to some forms of capitalism (where it is often possible to command ownership of natural resources) and to some forms of socialism (which is often thought to involve some kind of equalised control over the means of production). Rawls's argument is *not*, however, that such models of ownership would necessarily be *illegitimate*. His view is instead that we cannot consider their selection to be *basic* matters of justice and that they are therefore not relevant to the inviolable rights we find in the first principle. Rawls therefore leaves quite open exactly what the right to property mentioned in the first principle amounts to.

Property and distributive justice

What then, for Rawls, does the right to own property specified in the first principle actually entail, if it cannot house the characteristics that he excludes from it? We can approach this question by examining his broader understanding of a just economic regime. In the earlier expressions of his theory, Rawls expresses uncertainty about which economic system is best suited to realising his two principles of justice. Indeed, he often shows a conscious openness towards acceptable forms of economic organisation. In *A Theory of Justice*, for instance, Rawls claims that while justice does not absolutely require an equal right to participate in the control of the means of production within a society, it might nevertheless be *consistent* with it. This view would seem to imply that Rawls's liberal theory would be as compatible with socialism as with capitalism, which again suggests a less than steadfast commitment to private ownership despite the ostensible robustness of its presence in the first principle. This openness towards economic systems recedes slightly as Rawls continues to develop and articulate his theory over time. In his later writings, he is far clearer about his endorsement of one specific economic regime. He advocates what he calls a *property-owning democracy*, a term that he borrows from the economist James Meade (see O'Neill 2009). In his definition and defence of property-owning democracy, Rawls comes to insist that it is the *only* economic system capable of supporting his principles of justice.

It is important to emphasise that Rawls describes this economic regime – in which property ownership is evidently at the heart – explicitly as 'an *alternative* to capitalism' (2001: 135–6), rather than as any kind of interpretation of it. In making his case for property-owning democracy, Rawls rejects rival economic arrangements, including 'laissez-faire capitalism' and 'state socialism'. He dismisses laissez-faire capitalism – which he defines as a system where there is minimal state interference with the market economy – because it can at best assure merely formal, rather than the 'fair' equality of opportunity outlined in his second principle. Rawls's idea of fair equality of opportunity goes far beyond the colloquial understanding of the concept. For him, fair equality of opportunity demands more than an anti-discrimination principle ensuring that the distribution of goods or jobs are not linked to arbitrary criteria like gender or race. Although laissez-faire capitalism might be very friendly to a meritocratic demolition of these explicit discriminatory barriers, its hands-off interpretation of equality of opportunity pays no attention to the impedimentary role of economic and social disparities. Such disparities accompany significant intergenerational inequalities and threaten equal opportunities. If a person is born into the lowest socio-economic group within a society, or a group that has suffered historical marginalisation, they can find that this mere *fact about themselves* acts as a cultural barrier to economic success despite the absence of any *formal* discrimination against them. The thought is that under laissez-faire capitalism it would be eccentric to say that – recalling our Nozickean sports star example – Ronaldo's child and the child of one of his less wealthy spectators experience meaningful equality of opportunity when there is such a gulf between their material wealth and the advantages that it can secure. To achieve fair equality of opportunity we must instead design policies and institutions to overcome the disadvantages faced by many, perhaps through an appropriately egalitarian organisation and distribution of educational and cultural resources.

Rawls likewise rejects state socialism, on the grounds that the command economy it implies would necessarily violate the basic rights and freedoms that his first principle guarantees. In a command economy, where there is complete state control over economic affairs, the freedom of individuals to develop and pursue a plan for their lives would be denied and their ability to make meaningful choices about their work correspondingly thwarted. It would undermine the 'self-respect' that is definitive of Rawls's commitment to the moral sanctity of the individual. Even if such a centralised economic system were to be geared towards the promotion of some kind of egalitarian ideal, it would violate the fundamental rights that Rawls thinks we have as equal moral agents. After all, one of the main reasons Rawls gives for justifying the right to private property for each person is the connection between ownership and 'personal independence'. Part of what it means to be independent is to have the power to make appropriate choices about one's economic life, and having a right to property enables this important freedom.

Given his core moral commitments to both equality and freedom, it is perhaps not such a surprise that Rawls's theory of justice dismisses both an unfettered market and monolithic state control over the economy. It is more remarkable that he explicitly rejects what he calls 'welfare-state capitalism'. He frames his vision of property-owning democracy against welfare-state capitalism, though it is not immediately evident what the difference between these economic regimes amounts to. Within the political discourses of most putative social democracies, a concern with 'welfare' customarily refers to a

variety of state provisions that are supposed to aid those in
need and protect individuals and communities from experiences of hardship and poverty. Such a state commitment to
welfare thus implies a degree of progressive taxation, which
necessarily involves limitations to (or interference with) the
ownership of private property. These welfare arrangements
are often justified on the basis that they tame the excessive
inequalities that unfettered capitalism would permit. If an
individual in a capitalist economy experiences, for example,
unemployment because of a shift in consumer demand for
the goods she was involved in producing, the state can step
in to provide temporary assistance through the issuance of
funds. Such schemes help people when they suffer the various
problems thrown up by a functioning market economy.

For Rawls, such welfare-state capitalism is – in spite of
its redistributive commitments – insufficient for the vision
of fair equality of opportunity he endorses. It is insufficient
because it is inegalitarian and therefore undemocratic. As
an economic arrangement, welfare-state capitalism 'permits
very large inequalities in the ownership of real property
(productive assets and natural resources) so that the control
of the economy and much of political life rests in few hands'
(Rawls 2001: 138). Although it might protect individuals
who face circumstances of desperate need, by providing
them with sufficient resources to secure a certain level of
welfare, it still fails to treat citizens adequately as equals.
The economic inequalities that accompany welfare capitalism
lead to political inequalities through the concentration of
political power in the hands of the wealthy. Rawls does not
provide much in the way of detail about how this concentration of power manifests itself, but it can presumably
include a variety of practices. These could range from the
more blatant examples of the wealthy wielding influence
through large donations to political parties and campaigns,
to more insidious cases of exclusive institutions of educational and cultural privilege that enable elitist networks to
command informal influence over civic decisions.

What, though, does Rawls's idea of property-owning
democracy involve and what makes it superior to welfare-
state capitalism? In popular political discourse, the notion
of a property-owning democracy is one probably most often

associated with anti-statist policies. Indeed, according to one British historian, the term was 'one of the ideological and rhetorical constants of twentieth-century Conservatism' (Francis 2012: 275). First coined in the 1920s in the UK, by a Unionist MP, it was then prominent in Conservative Party policy discussions during the 1960s and was eventually invoked by Margaret Thatcher in the 1980s as the key privatising ideal to be contrasted with the socialist objective of extending public ownership wherever possible. Thatcher's ambitious – and popular – 'right to buy' scheme enabled the transfer of a huge amount of UK social housing stock from the state to private individuals at prices considerably lower than market value. Encouraging individuals and families to become property owners rather than rent their homes from a local political authority was a central part of her vision of rolling back the state. It was certainly not associated with any explicit aim to combat the inequalities associated with the market economy. It thus seems strange – given his commitment to fair equality of opportunity – that the concept of property-owning democracy has more appeal to Rawls than welfare-state capitalism.

Rawls's own philosophical account of property-owning democracy is strikingly different from the more politically familiar understanding common to opponents of public ownership. The definitive characteristic of his version is its emphasis on the role that economics can play in politics – and specifically on how the equality demanded by democracy dictates that property has a certain form. For Rawls,

> the background institutions of property-owning democracy work to *disperse* the ownership of wealth and capital, and thus to prevent a small part of society from controlling the economy, and indirectly, political life as well. By contrast, welfare-state capitalism permits a small class to have a near monopoly of the means of production. (2001: 139, emphasis added)

This passage makes plain Rawls's belief that the fundamental objective of property-owning democracy is quite distinct from that of welfare capitalism. The dispersal of economic and social power is a key aim – and thus not just an accidental by-product or secondary benefit – of property-owning democracy. Although welfare-state capitalism might be characterised by the aim to ameliorate poverty – and thus improve the material condition of the worst-off within a society, or reduce inequalities in resources – it has no corresponding interest in the dispersal of economic and social power. It protects people against material suffering from the worst excesses of capitalism, but it does nothing to guarantee that their equal political status is not undermined by the economic inequalities they experience. Welfare-state capitalism does not therefore go far enough to guarantee the protection of each person's self-respect and the other rights secured by Rawls's first principle.

Property-owning democracy and the concept of predistribution

Having established the objective that defines property-owning democracy – the assurance of meaningful political equality secured by the reduction of significant economic inequalities – we need now to understand the means by which Rawls thinks it achievable. We need to know how property-owning democracy works. Rawls puts forward the following description of the way in which it functions:

> Property-owning democracy avoids [a near monopoly of the means of production], not by the redistribution of income to those with less at the *end* of each period, so to speak, but rather by ensuring the widespread ownership of productive assets and human capital (that is, education and trained skills) at the *beginning* of each period, all this against a background of fair equality of opportunity. The intent is not simply to assist those who lose out through accident or misfortune (although that must be done), but rather to put all citizens in a position to manage their own affairs on a footing of a suitable degree of social and economic equality. (2001: 139, emphasis added)

This passage reveals one of the novel features of Rawls's idea: its requirement that the redistributive policies required by property-owning democracy should take place at the beginning of 'each period' (*ex ante*) rather than at the end (*ex post*). It is a theory of '*predistribution*' rather than merely redistribution. This idea of predistribution is evidently central to the distinctiveness of Rawls's understanding of property-owning democracy, but it needs further unpacking, not least because his own account is quite brief. There are three pertinent questions we can address to help us further understand what predistribution means: (1) why does it matter that the relevant distribution of property is established *ex ante* rather than *ex post*?; (2) what does such a predistribution then actually mean in practical, institutional, or policy terms?; and (3) what does the idea of predistribution mean for the right to private property that is observed by Rawls as part of the first principle of justice? Answering these questions will enable us to appreciate more fully how Rawls understands the concept of property and how individual rights to it fit within his theory of justice.

The answer to the first question – why *ex ante*? – harks back to the civic egalitarianism that underpins Rawls's idea of property-owning democracy. Under welfare-state capitalism, the state intervenes essentially as a force of *mitigation*. It provides a remedial resource that citizens need when their well-being is *already* threatened. It is, in this respect, a latent force. Its focus is therefore ultimately retrospective and, apart from a concern to overcome the problems generated by capitalism, the state is unconcerned with the *structural organisation* of an economy. Under property-owning democracy, by contrast, the state seeks to be not a latent but an *active* force, with a not retrospective but *prospective* focus, insofar as its intervention is designed not primarily to mitigate against misfortune (though this will be part of its role), but instead to, as far as possible, reduce or even prevent *future* inequalities from being severe. Whereas the distributive fallout of welfare-state capitalism is determined through apparent accident – through the combination of the unpredictable consequences arising from behaviour in the free market and the subsequent ameliorative responses from the state – the function of property-owning democracy is actually to *impose* an economic structure on society. The nature of this structure is essentially egalitarian and the reason that it is necessary relates to the *democratic* part of the society of property-owners that Rawls has in mind. His worry is that the sort of monopoly of wealth and resources that is left unchecked under welfare-state capitalism ends up distorting the democratic process, because with the possession of wealth comes political power. The wealthy are, through various means of acquiring influence and social capital, capable of excluding the economically worst off from the political process, and civic equality is thwarted as a result.[3]

We can also make sense of Rawls's argument in the Hegelian terms discussed in the previous chapter. The reason that Hegel rejects both state redistribution and charity is that both violate the agency of individuals. Being a passive recipient of resources without being part of the economic system through work or equivalent activity means being treated as a mere animal rather than as a conscious agent with consequent status in the world. On this Hegelian understanding, it demeans us to receive welfare from others. Although Rawls would surely not go as far as Hegel in this regard, the thought underpinning his account of economic justice has some similarities. Rawls's view is that the securement of our status as political equals within a community is better served through an *ex ante* structure that supports it, rather than an *ex post* attempt to revive this condition after it has been threatened by indigence. Such an attempted revival will be insufficient to recognise our moral status as equals. The fundamentally reactive nature of welfare-state capitalism fails to enable the needy individual to establish agency because, while it fulfils immediate material needs, it does not empower or promote self-respect. The aim of property-owning democracy is thus to disrupt (rather than mitigate) inequalities in political status through ensuring a fair distribution of all the sorts of resources that are conducive to a person's independence. Securing political equality through meaningful structural change explains why it matters that distributive initiatives from the state need to be *ex ante* rather than merely *ex post*.

Having identified why such an *ex ante* economic organisation matters, we can move on to the second question about the practical entailments of a politics of predistribution.

We already know that the institutions of property-owning democracy are set to disperse wealth and capital. They do so by placing the economic means of production 'in the hands of citizens generally'. Though this might seem, at first, to suggest the centralised state socialism that Rawls initially rejected, he has in mind not a command economy but rather a genuine democratisation of economic power. Rawls's own views about *how* to democratise the means of production are somewhat underdeveloped. He amplified his conviction about the rightness of property-owning democracy towards the end of his life, but his views on its practical implications lack detail. When he does contemplate the institutional requirements of this economic regime, he appears open-minded and flexible. For example, while he endorses certain forms of taxation, he signals that there may be contextual considerations that should inform practical deliberations and judgements on such issues. The same openness is visible in his view of worker-managed cooperative firms – an idea defended by Mill as well as Marx – which he suggests could be compatible with property-owning democracy, though would not be required by it (Rawls 2001: 176, 178). The absence of practical prescription in Rawls's theory provides a potentially useful framework for consideration of how best to think through the details of property-owning democracy. It also allows us to theorise about how best to organise our democratic systems to minimise the political influence of unaccountable economic elites.

Subsequent political philosophers have taken up the challenge of trying to work out precise policy initiatives to best realise Rawls's commitment to predistribution. The most comprehensive recent attempt has been Alan Thomas's *Republic of Equals* (2017). In the background of Thomas's analysis is the emergence of what he calls 'the new inequality' that has characterised Western liberal democracies since the late twentieth century and the 'drift to oligarchy' that such an economic context enables (2017: 10).[4] Thomas outlines what he thinks are the most effective policy implications of property-owning democracy, which 'ensure that all citizens have access to capital' (ix). Among the mechanisms he recommends for the required diffusion of capital across a society is the progressive taxation of wealth to address the fact that higher earners acquire a significantly larger proportion of their income from their capital rather than their labour (168–9). The possession of wealth – and its intergenerational transfer – solidifies the position of social elite networks and further cements economic and political inequalities. A focus on wealth rather than merely income is therefore important for the economic restructuring that property-owning democracy requires. As well as taxing wealth, Thomas suggests a 'society-wide unit trust' be established, which would be 'made up of a portfolio of equity held for all citizens by the state' (170). The intention behind this initiative is to empower citizens through securing them a stake in the economy and reconceiving state funding as an entitlement based on equal status rather than need. Related to this idea, Thad Williamson has further argued that one of the desirable ingredients of a property-owning democracy – to genuinely broaden the ownership of capital – would be universal access to a capital fund that could be used by individuals to invest in productive ventures (2014: 236–7). In each of these practical examples, the purpose of dispersing capital resources is a correspondingly democratic distribution of economic power along lines inspired by Rawls's theory.

While the precise policy implications of property-owning democracy seem open for fruitful contestation, Rawls's idea does face a basic challenge to its orientation. This challenge concerns the viability of the conceptual distinction between predistribution and redistribution. The problem is that the temporal relativity of the two terms suggests that they might actually be indistinguishable. In plainer terms, it seems that the categories of *ex ante* and *ex post* must always amount to the same thing; after all, whenever the relevant distributive activity is scheduled, it will inevitably take place *before* something and *after* something else. The various predistributive policies mentioned will necessarily take place against the backdrop of *some* history of economic activity. Rawls cannot think that any relevant policies will be enacted at some kind of new economic beginning for a society. Even if we were to establish an appropriate 'starting gate' for the initial *ex ante* distribution designed to capture economic fairness, any subsequent distributive activity – necessary to maintain the imposition of the structure of property-owning democracy – would seemingly be *ex post*. Is it not the case that what counts as *ex ante* at a certain time is necessarily *ex post* from the perspective of the previous time? If this is the case, is it possible to distinguish the two concepts meaningfully and, if not, does property-owning democracy lose its specificity?

This worry likely misunderstands the nature of predistribution, which is not really defined by a temporal contrast to the redistributive alternative, but rather by the difference in *purpose* already explained, which then requires substantive policies with distinct aims.[5] The definitive characteristic of a predistributive policy is that it is not merely ameliorative of inequalities as they arise within the marketplace, because such initiatives fail to attempt to prevent *future* inequalities. This failure seems implicit in the standard image of the 'safety net' for the needy that is characteristic of welfare-state capitalism. The very existence of a safety net assumes that people will fall at unpredictable times but ultimately be caught. The focus of predistributive policies is to alter the economic arrangements of a society to remove the need for such a comprehensive net, rather than to provide better reinforcements for it, or enable it to catch needy people more easily.

This predistributive structure of Rawls's theory fits with his commitment to intergenerational justice. He thinks that a liberal political community should adhere to a 'principle of just saving' (2001: 159–60), which obliges present generations to amass sufficient resources to sustain their successors. Present generations are thereby prevented from squandering their resources selfishly. Further provisions for intergenerational justice in his theory include various forms of taxation, with recommendations of significant regulation of bequest and inheritance (161). Rawls emphasises that the purpose of such taxation is not to empower the state, but rather to 'prevent accumulations of wealth that are judged to be inimical to background justice' (161). The thought is again that transmissions of intergenerational advantage will undermine the basic equality of citizens and vitiate the fair equality of opportunity principle. In endorsing these measures, Rawls does not think one generation simply replaces another at a certain point in time at which there needs to be distributive activity. As with the case of predistribution over redistribution, the idea of intergenerational justice reveals the *constant* nature of the state, acting to preserve property-owning democracy.

Having explained why predistribution matters and having offered some ideas as to what it might entail in practical terms, we can now move on to our third question, which is how Rawls's commitment to political equality – through the taxation of wealth and posthumous transfers, as well as establishing investment funds for citizens – fits with his stipulated right to basic property. How can Rawls defend a right to private property as part of his first principle of justice while at the same time advance an economic theory that places significant restrictions on that right, in the form of potentially significant taxation of acquired income and wealth and of transfers between individuals? These questions seem especially urgent since we have explained that what defines Rawls's theory against traditional redistributive alternatives is its ambition for the state to be constantly active, vigilant in its imposition of an economic structure. We might worry that his vision of property-owning democracy appears to recall the nightmarish scenario imagined by Nozick, where the state is required to intervene at all times to maintain a distributive pattern, such that it cannot tolerate capitalist acts between consenting adults.

If, however, we recall the nature of the right to property that Rawls observes, we can see that it fits quite neatly with his view of the state, and that it fuses together his commitments to freedom and equality. For him, the individual right to personal property is rooted in the need to secure 'personal independence and a sense of self-respect' (2001: 114). These values do not conflict with the predistributive character of property-owning democracy, which is geared towards taxation of the relatively wealthy, who will – it can be assumed – have a surfeit of the property holdings necessary to secure their independence and self-respect. The promise of predistribution is, moreover, the establishment of civic equality, which would seem to promote further the ends to be satisfied by the right to personal property – independence and self-respect – by ensuring that all enjoy them. The two components of Rawls's normative economic theory (the right to property, and predistribution within property-owning democracy) are thus mutually supportive of each other.

Conclusion

The manner in which Rawls's theory hangs together might persuade advocates of Nozickean libertarianism that property-owning democracy is something of a misnomer. It is certainly true that each theory understands the concept of *private ownership* very differently, which is another reminder of its fundamental contestability. For Nozick, private ownership implies full rights over holdings, whereas for Rawls, not only does it not include such powers, its justifiability is part of an overarching theory that actually implies the necessity of their *restriction*. The determination of which of the two conceptions is more compelling will depend on which of the key moral premises – self-ownership or civic equality – is preferred. Choosing between them is not, however, as innocent or as straightforward as nominating a favourite flavour of ice cream. Although debates in political philosophy are often marked by fierce contestation that can be boiled down to adherence to not only rival, but also incommensurable foundational principles, there are other ways of providing adjudication for disputes. One of these ways might be an acknowledgement of normative pluralism and of the corresponding view that among the virtues of a particular account of a concept will be its potential congruence with other values that we cherish. Property, as all the thinkers we have surveyed agree, is a very important concept, but it is not the only one in our normative arsenal.

Conclusion

It should by now be clear that it is hard to study property in isolation and that an appreciation of its contestation involves paying theoretical attention to other concepts. Perhaps such overlap is a feature of political theory as a field of inquiry that has few boundaries beyond those ephemeral ones created by clusters of scholars in conversation with each other. In the preceding discussions of different theories of property, I have focused chiefly on their entanglement with conceptual and normative contestations of freedom and equality, and have hardly made mention of other relevant ideas, such as power, democracy, and human rights. We have nevertheless traversed quite a lot of ground in a short space of time, moving swiftly through philosophical theories and arguments that often have their own significant scholarly literatures that are themselves replete with fascinating debates.

By way of conclusion, let me recall our steps and see where we have ended up. After briefly addressing the disagreements between contemporary philosophers about how best to conceptualise property, we moved on to discuss worries about its very existence. These worries – expressed by critics such as Rousseau and Proudhon – centred on the plight of those excluded or marginalised by the institution. These critics built their case against property on the claim that the institution of private ownership is the root cause of poverty and inequality in the modern world. Their critique invites us to take seriously the task of providing some kind of normative justification for this institution that we largely take for granted in Western liberal democracies. As we discovered, the history of modern political thought reveals that a significant number of important writers have been readily up for the task of justifying private property.

The arguments we have breezed through at high speed have ranged from the medieval theology of Thomas Aquinas to suggestions for economic organisation from twenty-first-century post-Rawlsians. We began with Nozick, because his libertarianism appears to house a very robust defence of private ownership rights, such that he considers them inviolable to all but the most minimal (and consensual) taxation by the state. We saw that the principle of self-ownership that undergirds his theory – as it must any such strong, non-consequentialist libertarianism – has morphed into something very different from the ancestral moral commitment we find in Locke's *Two Treatises*, the theological framework of which is part of a lineage of natural rights theories. These theories are rooted in a comprehensive normative understanding of natural law that simply could not entertain the kind of individualism we find in Nozick and contemporary libertarianism. Modern libertarians can shrug off the idea of obligations we might owe to others as easily as they can Locke's theological baggage, but, in doing so, they cannot explain why the freedom of a proprietor is more important than that of those who lack property.

It is, of course, possible to defend a consequentialist version of libertarianism, but this will, by its very nature, not yield a very robust justification of property as a social institution, because its legitimacy is vulnerable to collapse through any changes in empirical information. Appeals to consequentialism might have some plausibility in theoretical discussions of the arrangement or distribution of property, but they are of limited use to the justification of its very existence. Utilitarian theories certainly appeal to our intuitions that private property is justifiable because it serves the overall happiness or well-being of a society. But their reliance on notoriously ephemeral and contestable empirical phenomena weakens the otherwise impressive utilitarian theories of ownership that we looked at. The example of Bentham shows these limitations of utilitarianism: his theory is steadfastly committed to property, except in cases of emergency, when the state can justifiably interfere with it. While such an approach undoubtedly has an attractive dexterity, the resulting vulnerability of property will be unsatisfying to those in search of a more robust and principled philosophical case for the institution of private ownership.

Hegel's impressive account of property integrates a concern with it into a much broader theory of our reconciliation with the social and political world that surrounds us. His theory is attractively systematic and accords property a central place. It offers a compelling account of how property is necessary for the securement of the network of rights that gives concrete form to our personalities and provides meaningful freedom for individuals in a social context. Hegel is nevertheless unable to square this commitment to property with his contempt for those who happen to end up without it, in particular the rabble that he thinks are beyond salvation. Extreme poverty looks like a strange blind spot for him when viewed with twenty-first-century eyes. Those attracted to the justificatory part of the Hegelian story might therefore be very sympathetic to Rawls's vision of property-owning democracy. Rawls's theory embeds the idea of property within a broader theory of justice. The fact that he does not offer a discrete justification of private ownership that can be isolated from this theory enables him to avoid many of the pitfalls faced by the other accounts considered in previous chapters. This approach also allows him to offer a proper response to the case against property advanced in the first chapter, as it takes seriously worries about intergenerational inequalities in a structured way. In Rawls's theory, property emerges as a vital concept, but one that is a particular part of a holistically crafted normative vision. We have thus ended up where many conversations within contemporary political philosophy do: with renewed attention to a framework for political theory that has gripped practitioners of the discipline for fifty years. Though such a framework was long thought to relegate the idea of property ownership, on closer inspection, it turns out to place it at the heart of its theory.

Notes

Introduction: What is Property?

1 Alternative theoretical introductions to the concept of property include Becker 1977; Ryan 1984; Reeve 1986; and, more historically Garnsey 2007. Full-length philosophical analyses include Munzer 1990; Penner 1997, 2020; Harris 2002, as well as the recent discussion – as part of a larger consideration of human rights – in Cruft 2019. For an excellent recent history of the idea of property that covers far more than this book can, see the three volumes by Christopher Pierson (2013, 2016, 2020). To my mind, the most creative and rigorous discussion of property within contemporary political theory remains Waldron 1988.

2 See Pettit 1999 for elaboration of this thesis, as well as Skinner 2002.

3 For an illuminating full-length consideration of historical and contemporary philosophical accounts of bequest, see Halliday 2018. For further discussion, see also Braun 2010 and Lamb 2014.

4 For a comprehensive analysis that defends this view of property as a misleading concept, see Glackin 2014.

5 For a compelling philosophical account of the nature of intellectual traditions, see Bevir 1999.

1 The Case against Private Property

1 For a comprehensive philosophical exploration of Rousseau's *Discourse* and his arguments about inequality therein, see Neuhouser 2014.
2 For discussion of Locke's political writing (including his theory of property) in the context of colonialism, see Arneil 1996.
3 For discussions of Proudhon's broader political thought, see Ritter 1969 and Prichard 2013.
4 For discussions of Morris's broader political thought, see Thompson 1977 and Kinna 2000.

2 Libertarianism and the Natural Right to Property

1 For further reading on Nozick's libertarianism, two collections of useful essays on *Anarchy, State, and Utopia* are Paul 1982 and Bader and Meadowcroft 2011. Wolff 1991 provides a thorough full-length examination.
2 For a detailed explication of this view, see Steiner 1994: 6–54.
3 Kant's own theory of property is ultimately rather unclear on the question of whether the state has a duty to support the poor through the taxation of property. For different interpretations of Kant's somewhat ambiguous position expressed in his 'Doctrine of Right', see Weinrib 2002–3; Ripstein 2009; and Penner 2010.
4 For Cohen, 'Libertarians want to say that [1] interferences with people's use of their private property are unacceptable because they are, quite obviously, abridgements of freedom, *and* [2] that the reason why protection of private property does not similarly abridge the freedom of non-owners is that owners have a right to exclude others from their property and non-owners consequently have no right to use it. But they can say both things only if they define freedom in incompatible ways' (1995: 60).
5 It is, in any case, the everyday understanding that Nozick employs in *Anarchy, State, and Utopia*.
6 The scholarly literature on Locke's theory of property is vast. Among the most significant readings of his logic of justification for acquisition and ownership are Tully 1980; Waldron 1988; Simmons 1992; and Sreenivasan 1995.

3 Natural Law and the Gnarled Roots of Self-Ownership

1   Elsewhere in the text, Locke repeats his view that the rule that 'all, as much as may be, should be preserved' is 'the Fundamental Law of Nature' (1988: 391).

2   For the history of theories of natural rights, see especially Tuck 1979 and Tierney 1997.

3   For detailed discussion of the medieval roots of this idea, see Swanson 1997.

4   This obligation also includes numerous provisos. These include that we should have exhausted all other ways of satisfying our urgent need, that the owner will not himself subsequently be left in such a situation following our action, and that there is restitution planned for some stage in the future (Pufendorf 1991: 55–6).

5   For further discussion of the potential ambiguities in Locke's passage, see Lamb and Thompson 2009.

6   For compelling readings that stress the role that religion plays in Locke's political thought, see Dunn 1969 and Waldron 2003.

7   He does not explain why he turns to Locke at this point, beyond the fact that he is using a Lockean framework for his theory.

8   Some philosophers have called these theories 'left-libertarian', but this strikes me as an unhelpful label, since one of the key roles of scholarship is to dissuade students (and others) from thinking of political ideas along a simplistic spectrum – that runs from left to right – rather than to reify that notion and thus give it credibility.

9   For a fuller account of Paine's theory of property and the redistributive rights that it involves, as well as the reasons that he should ultimately not be considered a libertarian thinker, see Lamb 2015. For discussion of Paine's *Agrarian Justice* in a broader historical context, see Claeys 1994 and Stedman Jones 2004.

10   E.g. Otsuka 2003. See also the contributions to Steiner and Vallentyne 2000, 2001.

11   Feminist political theory provides powerful rejections of thinking of rights in terms of property. Several feminist theorists resist the notions that private ownership could ever capture the nature and character of our rights, that we should regard our rights as having normative priority over the inescapable duties of care that we have to others, and that we should countenance the notion that our bodies are marketable commodities. See,

for example, the penetrating analysis in Phillips 2013. See also Pateman 2002, who likewise concludes that the idea of 'property in the person' (her preferred term for self-ownership) 'must be left behind' (52) for the sake of meaningful democracy. For a critical engagement that draws on feminist insights to reconceive an alternative, 'connected' conception of self-ownership, see Cudd 2019.

4 Property for the Greater Good: Utilitarian Theories of Ownership

1   For a good discussion of Hume's place within the utilitarian tradition, see Rosen 2003. For broader analyses of Hume's political theory, see McArthur 2007 and Sabl 2012.
2   For further discussion of Bentham's broader political theory, see Kelly 1990 and Schofield 2006.
3   For further discussion of Bentham's account of property and the role that his disappointment prevention principle plays within it, see Long 1979 and Kelly 1990.
4   The literature on Mill's political philosophy is huge. Among the instructive full-length philosophical studies are Donner 1993; Miller 2010; and Brink 2013. Several of the essays in Skorupski 1998 also address his moral and political philosophy.
5   Mill's sympathy to socialist ideas increased during his lifetime. For discussions of his liberal socialism, see Claeys 1987; Miller 2003; and Medearis 2005, as well as Mill's (1994b) own 'Chapters on Socialism', published posthumously in 1879.
6   Whereas Bentham's theory is committed to an ultimately subjective understanding of individual pleasure, Mill's utilitarianism is teleological, with a perfectionist human end as its aim. In *On Liberty*, Mill defends the individual right to unimpeded thought and expression with reference to this teleological understanding (of 'utility in the largest sense'), which he more fully outlines in his essay *Utilitarianism* and other writings.
7   His full definition is: 'The institution of property, when limited to its essential elements, consists in the recognition, in each person, of a right to the exclusive disposal of what he or she have produced by their own exertions, or received either by gift or by fair agreement, without force or fraud, from those who produced it' (Mill 1994a: 25).
8   For a more detailed account of Mill's views on posthumous transfers of property, see Halliday 2018: 47–57.

5 Ownership as Will in the World: Hegel's Account of Property

1   The most comprehensive introduction to Hegel's political thought that I have encountered is Knowles 2002. See also Hampsher-Monk 1992: 409–82; Hardimon 1994; and Patten 1999 for insightful discussions of how his politics fits into his broader philosophy.
2   As with the majority of contributors to modern Western political thought, he does not regard non-human animals as rights holders, a position that he justifies through reference to their lack of self-consciousness (revealed, among other things, by their alleged inability to destroy themselves) (Hegel 1991: 78).
3   We are therefore not permitted to alienate our personalities by contracting into arrangements that involve 'slavery, serfdom, disqualification from owning property, restrictions on freedom of ownership, etc.' (Hegel 1991: 96).
4   For further discussion of this issue, see Teichgraeber 1977. See also Whitt 2013, who argues that the fate of the rabble does not reveal, in fact, a failure on Hegel's part, because his vision of the modern state is one that depends on the persistence of poverty and the corresponding denial of freedom to some.

6 Property within Justice: Rawls and Beyond

1   There is a gargantuan and ever-growing literature on Rawls. For perhaps the most comprehensive exposition of his political thought, see Freeman 2007.
2   We do perhaps find echoes of Mill's attitude to land in Rawls's exclusion of natural resources.
3   Economist James Meade (1964) also eloquently expresses the worry that inequalities in property then entail civic or political inequalities. As O'Neill 2009 and 2020 points out, Rawls's account of property-owning democracy is indebted to Meade, though there are also some important differences between the two.
4   In advancing his account of property-owning democracy, Thomas invokes the pioneering economic analysis of Thomas Piketty (2014), which charts the massive increases in wealth

inequality in recent years. For discussion of the broader relevance of Piketty's work for political philosophy (particularly in relation to Rawls's theory), see O'Neill 2017.

5 See O'Neill 2020 for a thorough analysis of the logics of various redistributive and predistributive economic policies that likewise reaches this conclusion about the relevant conceptual distinction lying in their *aims*.

Bibliography

Amis, Martin (1995) *The Information*. London: Flamingo.

Aquinas, Thomas (2002) *Political Writings*, ed. R. W. Dyson. Cambridge: Cambridge University Press.

Arneil, Barbara (1996) *John Locke and America: The Defence of English Colonialism*. Oxford: Clarendon Press.

Bader, Ralf and Meadowcroft, John (2011) *The Cambridge Companion to Robert Nozick's 'Anarchy, State, and Utopia'*. Cambridge: Cambridge University Press.

Becker, Lawrence (1977) *Property Rights: Philosophic Foundations*. London: Routledge & Kegan Paul.

Bentham, Jeremy (2001 [1843]) 'Principles of the Civil Code' in R. Harrison (ed.) *Bentham: Selected Writings on Utilitarianism*. London: Wordsworth, pp. 313–80.

Bevir, Mark (1999) *The Logic of the History of Ideas*. Cambridge: Cambridge University Press.

Braun, Stewart S. (2010) 'Historical Entitlement and the Practice of Bequest: Is there a Moral Right of Bequest?' *Law and Philosophy* 29: 6, 695–715.

Brennan, Jason and van der Vossen, Bas (2017) 'The Myths of the Self-Ownership Thesis' in J. Brennan, B. van der Vossen, and D. Schmidtz (eds.) *The Routledge Handbook of Libertarianism*. New York: Routledge, pp. 199–211.

Brink, David (2013) *Mill's Progressive Principles*. Oxford: Oxford University Press.

Claeys, Gregory (1987) 'Justice, Independence, and Industrial Democracy: The Development of John Stuart Mill's Views on Socialism'. *The Journal of Politics* 49: 1, 122–47.

Claeys, Gregory (1994) 'The Origins of the Rights of Labor: Republicanism and Commerce in Britain, 1796–1805'. *Journal of Modern History* 66: 2, 249–90.

Cohen, G. A. (1995) *Self-Ownership, Freedom, and Equality*. Cambridge: Cambridge University Press.

Cruft, Rowan (2019) *Human Rights, Ownership, and the Individual*. Oxford: Oxford University Press.

Cudd, Ann E. (2019) 'Connected Self-Ownership and our Obligations to Others'. *Social Philosophy and Policy* 36: 2, 154–73.

Demsetz, Harold (1967) 'Towards a Theory of Property Rights', *The American Economic Review* 57: 2, 347–59.

Donner, Wendy (1993) *The Liberal Self: John Stuart Mill's Moral and Political Philosophy*. Ithaca, NY: Cornell University Press.

Dunn, John (1969) *The Political Thought of John Locke: An Historical Account of the Argument of the 'Two Treatises of Government'*. Cambridge: Cambridge University Press.

Filmer, Robert (2008 [1680]) *Patriarcha and Other Writings*, ed. J. P. Somerville. Cambridge: Cambridge University Press.

Francis, Matthew (2012) '"A Crusade to Enfranchise the Many": Thatcherism and the "Property-Owning Democracy"'. *Twentieth-Century British History* 23: 2, 275–97.

Freeman, Samuel (2007) *Rawls*. Abingdon: Routledge.

Garnsey, Peter (2007) *Thinking about Property: From Antiquity to the Age of Revolution*. Cambridge: Cambridge University Press.

Glackin, Shane (2014) 'Back to Bundles: Deflating Property Rights, Again'. *Legal Theory* 20: 1, 1–24.

Grotius, Hugo (1925 [1625]) *The Law of War and Peace*, ed. James Scott Brown. Oxford: Clarendon Press.

Halliday, Daniel (2018) *The Inheritance of Wealth: Justice, Equality, and the Right to Bequeath*. Oxford: Oxford University Press.

Hampsher-Monk, Iain (1992) *A History of Modern Political Thought: Major Political Thinkers from Hobbes to Marx*. Oxford: Basil Blackwell.

Hardimon, Michael (1994) *Hegel's Social Philosophy: The Project of Reconciliation*. Cambridge: Cambridge University Press.

Harris, J. W. (2002) *Property and Justice*. Oxford: Oxford University Press.

Hegel, G. W. F. (1991 [1820]) *Elements of the Philosophy of Right*, ed. A. W. Wood. Cambridge: Cambridge University Press.

Hohfeld, Wesley Newcomb (1919) *Fundamental Legal Conceptions*, ed. W. Cook. New Haven: Yale University Press.

Honoré, Anthony (1993 [1961]) 'Ownership' in Patricia Smith

(ed.) *The Nature and Process of Law: An Introduction to Legal Philosophy*. Oxford: Oxford University Press, pp. 370–5.

Hume, David (1978 [1739]) *A Treatise of Human Nature*, P. H. Nidditch. Oxford: Clarendon Press.

Kelly, Paul J. (1990) *Utilitarianism and Distributive Justice: Jeremy Bentham and the Civil Law*. Oxford: Clarendon Press.

Kinna, Ruth (2000) *William Morris and the Art of Socialism*. Cardiff: University of Wales Press.

Knowles, Dudley (2002) *Hegel and the Philosophy of Right*. London: Routledge.

Lamb, Robert (2014) 'The Power to Bequeath'. *Law and Philosophy* 33: 5, 629–54.

Lamb, Robert (2015) *Thomas Paine and the Idea of Human Rights*. Cambridge: Cambridge University Press.

Lamb, Robert and Thompson, Benjamin (2009) 'The Meaning of Charity in Locke's Political Thought'. *European Journal of Political Theory* 8: 2, 229–52.

Locke, John (1988 [1689]) *Two Treatises of Government*, ed. P. Laslett. Cambridge: Cambridge University Press.

Long, Douglas G. (1979) 'Bentham on Property' in Thomas M. Flanagan and Anthony Parel (eds.) *Theories of Property: Aristotle to the Present*. Waterloo: Wilfred Laurier University Press, pp. 221–54.

McArthur, Neil (2007) *David Hume's Political Theory: Law, Commerce, and the Constitution of Government*. Toronto: University of Toronto Press.

Mack, Eric (2018) *Libertarianism*. Cambridge: Polity.

Marx, Karl (1972a) 'Society and Economy in History' in Robert C. Tucker (ed.) *The Marx-Engels Reader*. London: W. W. Norton & Company, pp. 136–42.

Marx, Karl (1972b [1932]), 'The German Ideology' in Robert C. Tucker (ed.) *The Marx-Engels Reader*. London: W. W. Norton & Company, pp. 146–200.

Marx, Karl, and Engels, Friedrich (1972c [1848]) 'The Manifesto of the Communist Party' in Robert C. Tucker (ed.) *The Marx-Engels Reader*. London: W. W. Norton & Company, pp. 469–500.

Meade, James (1964) *Efficiency, Equality and the Ownership of Property*. London: George Allen & Unwin.

Medearis, John (2005) 'Labor, Democracy, Utility, and Mill's Critique of Private Property'. *American Journal of Political Science* 49: 1, 135–49.

Mill, John Stuart (1994a [1848]) 'Principles of Political Economy' in Jonathan Riley (ed.) *'Principles of Political Economy' and*

'*Chapters on Socialism*'. Oxford: Oxford University Press, pp. 1–367.

Mill, John Stuart (1994b [1879]) 'Chapters on Socialism' in Jonathan Riley (ed.) '*Principles of Political Economy*' *and* '*Chapters on Socialism*'. Oxford: Oxford University Press, pp. 369–436.

Miller, Dale (2003) 'Mill's "Socialism"'. *Politics, Philosophy, and Economics* 2: 2, 213–38.

Miller, Dale (2010) *J. S. Mill: Moral, Social, and Political Thought*. Cambridge: Polity.

Morris, William (2003 [1890]) *News from Nowhere*, ed. D. Leopold. Oxford: Oxford University Press.

Munzer, Stephen (1990) *A Theory of Property*. Cambridge: Cambridge University Press.

Murphy, Liam and Nagel, Thomas (2002) *The Myth of Ownership: Taxes and Justice*. Oxford: Oxford University Press.

Nagel, Thomas (1975) 'Libertarianism without Foundations'. *The Yale Law Journal* 85: 1, 136–49.

Narveson, Jan (2001 [1988]) *The Libertarian Idea*. Letchworth: Broadview Press.

Neuhouser, Frederick (2014) *Rousseau's Critique of Inequality: Reconstructing the Second Discourse*. Cambridge: Cambridge University Press.

Nozick, Robert (1974) *Anarchy, State, and Utopia*. Oxford: Blackwell.

O'Neill, Martin (2009) 'Liberty, Equality and Property-Owning Democracy'. *Journal of Social Philosophy* 40: 3, 379–96.

O'Neill, Martin (2017) 'Philosophy and Public Policy after Piketty'. *Journal of Political Philosophy* 25: 3, 343–75.

O'Neill, Martin (2020) 'Power, Predistribution, and Social Justice'. *Philosophy* 95: 1, 63–91.

Otsuka, Michael (2003) *Libertarianism without Inequality*. Oxford: Oxford University Press.

Paine, Thomas (1969 [1797]) 'Agrarian Justice' in Philip S. Foner (ed.) *The Complete Writings of Thomas Paine*. New York: Citadel Press, pp. 606–20.

Pateman, Carole (2002) 'Self-Ownership and Property in the Person: Democratization and a Tale of Two Concepts'. *The Journal of Political Philosophy* 10: 1, 20–53.

Patten, Alan (1999) *Hegel's Idea of Freedom*. Oxford: Oxford University Press.

Paul, Jeffrey (ed.) (1982) *Reading Nozick: Essays on 'Anarchy, State, and Utopia'*. Oxford: Blackwell.

Penner, James (1997) *The Idea of Property in Law*. Oxford: Clarendon Press.

Penner, James (2010) 'The State's Duty to Support the Poor in Kant's *Doctrine of Right*'. *British Journal of Politics and International Relations* 12: 1, 88–110.

Penner, James (2020) *Property Rights: A Re-examination*. Oxford: Oxford University Press.

Pettit, Phillip (1999) *Republicanism: A Theory of Freedom and Government*. Oxford: Oxford University Press.

Phillips, Anne (2013) *Our Bodies, Whose Property?* Princeton, NJ: Princeton University Press.

Pierson, Christopher (2013) *Just Property: A History in the Latin West, Volume 1: Wealth, Virtue, and the Law*. Oxford: Oxford University Press.

Pierson, Christopher (2016) *Just Property, Volume 2: Enlightenment, Revolution, and History*. Oxford: Oxford University Press.

Pierson, Christopher (2020) *Just Property, Volume 3: Property in an Age of Ideologies*. Oxford: Oxford University Press.

Piketty, Thomas (2014) *Capital in the Twenty-First Century*, trans. A. Goldhammer. Cambridge, MA: Harvard University Press.

Prichard, Alex (2013) *Justice, Order, and Anarchy: The International Political Theory of Pierre-Joseph Proudhon*. Abingdon: Routledge.

Proudhon, Pierre-Joseph (1994 [1840]), *What is Property?*, ed. D. R. Kelley and B. G. Smith. Cambridge: Cambridge University Press.

Pufendorf, Samuel (1991 [1673]) *On the Duty of Man and the Citizen*, ed. J. Tully. Cambridge: Cambridge University Press.

Rawls, John (1999 [1971]) *A Theory of Justice*. Oxford: Oxford University Press.

Rawls, John (2001) *Justice as Fairness: A Restatement*. Cambridge, MA: Belknap Press.

Reeve, Andrew (1986) *Property*. London: Palgrave Macmillan.

Ripstein, Arthur (2009) *Force and Freedom: Kant's Legal and Political Philosophy*. Cambridge, MA: Harvard University Press.

Ritter, Alan (1969) *The Political Thought of Pierre-Joseph Proudhon*. Princeton, NJ: Princeton University Press.

Rosen, Frederick (2003) *Classical Utilitarianism from Hume to Mill*. London: Routledge.

Rousseau, Jean-Jacques (1997a [1755]) 'Discourse on the Origin and Foundations of Inequality Among Men' in V. Gourevitch (ed.), *Rousseau: The Discourses and Other Early Political Writings*. Cambridge: Cambridge University Press, pp. 111–222.

Rousseau, Jean-Jacques (1997b [1762]) 'The Social Contract' in V. Gourevitch (ed.), *Rousseau: The Social Contract and Other*

Later Political Writings. Cambridge: Cambridge University Press, pp. 39–153.

Ryan, Alan (1984) *Property and Political Theory*. Oxford: Basil Blackwell.

Sabl, Andrew (2012) *Hume's Politics: Coordination and Crisis in the 'History of England'*. Princeton, NJ: Princeton University Press.

Schofield, Philip (2006) *Utility and Democracy: The Political Thought of Jeremy Bentham*. Oxford: Oxford University Press.

Simmons, A. John (1992) *The Lockean Theory of Rights*. Princeton, NJ: Princeton University Press.

Skinner, Quentin (2002) 'A Third Concept of Liberty'. *Proceedings of the British Academy* 117, 237–68.

Skorupski, John (1998) *The Cambridge Companion to Mill*. Cambridge: Cambridge University Press.

Smith, Adam (1978) *Lectures on Jurisprudence: Report of 1762–63*, ed. R. L. Meek, D. D. Raphael, and P. G. Stein. Oxford: Liberty Fund.

Sreenivasan, Gopal (1995) *The Limits of Lockean Rights in Property*. Oxford: Oxford University Press.

Stedman Jones, Gareth (2004) *An End to Poverty? An Historical Debate*. London: Profile.

Steiner, Hillel (1994) *An Essay on Rights*. Oxford: Blackwell.

Steiner, Hillel and Vallentyne, Peter (eds.) (2000) *The Origins of Left-Libertarianism: An Anthology of Historical Writings*. London: Palgrave Macmillan.

Steiner, Hillel and Vallentyne, Peter (eds.) (2001) *Left-Libertarianism and its Critics: The Contemporary Debate*. London: Palgrave Macmillan.

Swanson, Scott G. (1997) 'The Medieval Foundations of John Locke's Theory of Natural Rights: Rights of Subsistence and the Principle of Extreme Necessity'. *History of Political Thought* 18: 3, 399–459.

Teichgraeber, Richard (1977) 'Hegel on Property and Poverty'. *Journal of the History of Ideas* 38: 1, 47–64.

Thomas, Alan (2017) *Republic of Equals: Predistribution and Property-Owning Democracy*. Oxford: Oxford University Press.

Thompson, E. P. (1977) *William Morris: Romantic to Revolutionary*. London: The Merlin Press.

Tierney, Brian (1997) *The Idea of Natural Rights*. Atlanta: Scholars Press for Emory University.

Tuck, Richard (1979) *Natural Rights Theories: Their Origin and Development*. Cambridge: Cambridge University Press.

Tully, James (1980) *A Discourse on Property: John Locke and his Adversaries*. Cambridge: Cambridge University Press.

Vallentyne, Peter (2018) 'Libertarianism and Taxation' in M. O'Neill and S. Orr (eds.) *Taxation: Philosophical Perspectives*. Oxford: Oxford University Press, pp. 98–110.

Van Parijs, Philippe (1995) *Real Freedom for All: What (if Anything) can Justify Capitalism?* Oxford: Oxford University Press.

Waldron, Jeremy (1988) *The Right to Private Property*. Oxford: Clarendon Press.

Waldron, Jeremy (2003) *God, Locke, and Equality: Christian Foundations in John Locke's Political Philosophy*. Cambridge: Cambridge University Press.

Weinrib, Ernest (2002–3) 'Poverty and Property Rights in Kant's System of Rights'. *Notre Dame Law Review* 78, 795–828.

Whitt, Matt S. (2013) 'The Problem of Poverty and the Limits of Freedom in Hegel's Theory of the Ethical State'. *Political Theory* 41: 2, 257–84.

Williamson, Thad (2014) 'Realizing Property-Owning Democracy: A 20-Year Strategy to Create an Egalitarian Distribution of Assets in the United States' in Martin O'Neill and Thad Williamson (eds.) *Property-Owning Democracy: Rawls and Beyond*. Chichester: Wiley Blackwell, pp. 225–48.

Wolff, Jonathan (1991) *Robert Nozick: Property, Justice, and the Minimal State*. Cambridge: Polity.

Index